MY ANCESTRY: THE CHILDREN

FOREVER FRIENDS

MIKE & FRIEND

Artful Memories

by Carol Wingert and Tena Sprenger

NORTH LIGHT BOOKS
CINCINNATI, OHIO
www.artistsnetwork.com

Dedication

We would like to dedicate this book to our spouses and children. Your support, encouragement, feedback and enthusiasm are totally appreciated. We are grateful that you ate many cardboard-flavored frozen dinners and take-out fast foods without complaint. You are our major reasons for being passionate about memory art.

Acknowledgments

We would like to say thanks to our editor, Jessica Gordon, and to Marissa Bowers and Christine Polomsky at F+W Publications, for your guidance and support, your professionalism and your warmth. You have made this project such a delight for us. And, to Christine Doyle, a special thanks for your confidence in us and in this project. Thank you also to our designers, Davis and Cindy Stanard; to page make-up artist, Kathy Gardner; and to our production coordinator, Greg Nock. Laurie Stamas and Kimberly Kwan, thanks to both of you for the bio photos. We love how you worked your magic.

Thank you also to our contributing guest artists for their creativity and willingness to share their passion.

Finally, we thank you, our readers, for being the inspiration for us to extend our artistic boundaries. Without you, there would be no reason for us to create this book.

Artful Memories. Copyright © 2006 by Carol Wingert and Tena Sprenger. Manufactured in the U.S.A. All rights reserved. The patterns and drawings in the book are for personal use of reader. By permission of the author and publisher, they may be either hand-traced or photocopied to make single copies, but under no circumstances may they be resold or republished. It is permissible for the purchaser to make the projects contained herein and sell them at fairs, bazaars and craft shows. No other part of this book may be reproduced in any form or by any electronic or mechanical means including information storage and retrieval systems without permission in writing from the publisher, except by a reviewer, who may quote a brief passage in review. Published by North Light Books, an imprint of F+W Publications, Inc., 4700 East Galbraith Road, Cincinnati, Ohio 45236. (800) 289-0963. First edition.

10 09 08 07 06   5 4 3 2 1

Library of Congress Cataloging-in-Publication Data
Wingert, Carol.
    Artful memories / Carol Wingert and Tena Sprenger.
        p. cm.
    Includes index.
    ISBN-13: 978-1-58180-810-0 (alk. paper)
    ISBN-10: 1-58180-810-0
1. Photograph albums. 2. Photographs--Conservation and restoration.
3. Scrapbooks. I. Sprenger, Tena. II. Title.
    TR501.W56 2006
    745.593--dc22
                    2006000803

fw
F+W PUBLICATIONS, INC.

Distributed in Canada by Fraser Direct
100 Armstrong Avenue
Georgetown, ON, Canada L7G 5S4
Tel: (905) 877-4411

Distributed in the U.K. and Europe by David & Charles
Brunel House, Newton Abbot, Devon, TQ12 4PU, England
Tel: (+44) 1626 323200, Fax: (+44) 1626 323319
Email: mail@davidandcharles.co.uk

Distributed in Australia by Capricorn Link
P.O. Box 704, S. Windsor, NSW 2756 Australia
Tel: (02) 4577-3555

Editor: Jessica Gordon
Designers: Davis and Cindy Stanard and Marissa Bowers
Layout Artist: Kathy Gardner
Production Coordinator: Greg Nock
Photographers: Christine Polomsky, Jennifer Reeves and Ken Trujillo
Stylist: Kevin Hardiek

About the Authors

Carol Wingert is a passionate memory and book arts instructor who teaches classes both nationally and internationally. Her international experiences include acting as the keynote guest "tutor" at a 2004 scrapbook convention in Australia. She has also taught at Creating Keepsakes University. In addition to teaching across the country, she is an instructor at her local stamping store, Ink It! Inc. She was lead artist for Autumn Leaves' *The Book Book* and has been a contributing artist in six of its other publications, including *Designing with Photos* and *Designing with Words*. Carol's art appears in a number of books published by Design Originals and she is also a frequent contributor to *Legacy* magazine. Carol lives in Gilbert, Arizona, with her husband Vern, daughter Ashley, and their menagerie of animals. In addition to her love of paper arts, Carol enjoys reading, gardening, cooking and traveling.

Tena Sprenger has always loved creative arts and teaching, and combining the two has created her dream job! Tena is an instructor at her local scrapbook store, Scrapbooks, Etc. She has also taught throughout the United States as well as internationally. Tena was recognized in 2003 as an honorable mention in the Creating Keepsakes Hall of Fame contest, and she was inducted into the Creating Keepsakes Hall of Fame in 2004. Tena's artwork is regularly featured in *Creating Keepsakes Magazine*. Tena has also been a contributing artist in *The Book Book*, *Designing with Fabric*, *Designing with Stamps* and *Designing with Paper*. Tena lives in Mesa, Arizona, with her husband Mike and her children, Alyssa and Michael. When Tena is not busy making a creative mess in her art room, she enjoys reading and dance.

What's Inside

Art for Memory's Sake	**7**
Art Supplies	**8**

Paper Arts — 12
Flip-Flop Girls	14
Forever Friends	16
Steven and Mr. Gecko	20
Love...by Example	22
Imperial Beach	24
My Tribute to Grandpop	26
Generations	30
Little Things	32
Family 4 Each Other	34
Paper Arts Gallery	38

Fabric Arts — 44
Family	46
I Love...	48
Summer Memories	50
Yes, You Are a Princess	52
My Ancestry: the Children	54
Fabric Arts Gallery	58

Book Arts — 60
100% You	62
Organized Chaos	64
Family Deck	68
This and That	70
She's Got Hatitude!	74
Oh, Bandana!	78
The Love of Color	82
Imagine	86
Entrances	90
Book Arts Gallery	94

Wall Arts — 98
Ilse and the Lion Cub	100
Life	102
The Arboretum	104
Samantha	106
Cousins	108
She's All Girl	112
Shy Beauty	114
Wall Arts Gallery	118

About Our Guest Artists	**121**
Bookmaking Techniques	**122**
Resources	**124**
Index	**126**

Art for Memory's Sake

When we refer to ourselves as memory artists, people often ask us what we mean. While we may not quite fit into the category of traditional artists, what we love to do is mesh our memory keeping with artistic techniques. Creatively displaying photos and enhancing them with materials and mediums often used by traditional artists is our favorite way to artistically express ourselves.

Perhaps the most important thing to us about our artwork is that it conveys heartfelt meaning. We agree with English poet Samuel Taylor Coleridge, who once said, "What comes from the heart, goes to the heart." The expression of emotion in our work distinguishes what we do from a craft. We interpret our memories through the colors we use, the mood or tone we set and the formats and styles we choose. We also often include the story behind the photo by adding journaling.

Each new project usually begins with a photo, a strong emotional feeling about a person or an event, or a need to document and remember something that has happened or is happening in our lives. The creative interpretation—the fun and rewarding part—comes next. Playing with supplies, colors, techniques and embellishments is a little like going back to grade school and messing with finger paints and clay. Finally, we "circle the table," taking a step back from our work to look at it from all angles. Both of us need to have the time for our minds to accept what we did as visually appealing and complete—to make sure that what we

wake up with in the morning looks as good as what we went to bed with the night before. Whatever your creative process may be, we hope that you enjoy playing and "messing" as much as we do.

Artful Memories is divided into four chapters: Paper Arts, Fabric Arts, Book Arts and Wall Arts. Each chapter will give you new ideas about how to create your own memory art, from sophisticated paper and fabric layouts to adorable mini books and original artwork to hang in your home. We love having people *oooh* and *aaah* over our handmade artwork, and we are excited to share some of our favorite projects with you.

Our hope is that this book will become a well-used, dog-eared and tattered favorite in your library. We want you to feel inspired to create, to look at what we did and say to yourself, "What if I did…?" It thrills us to know that you are experimenting with new materials and spending time in the art supply aisles getting lots of great ideas. We wait for "aha" moments, when we discover that sometimes very fun and funky projects can come from readily available materials and that creative expression does not necessarily mean many, many hours of labor. We hope this book sends you on your way to experiencing your own lightbulb moments. We are all about ditching the rules, experimenting with new materials and going beyond previously set artistic boundaries.

So, from our hearts to your heart, we wish you many artistic, inspirational, creative and messy moments.

Art Supplies

Paper

There is a vast amount of paper products to choose from when creating memory art. In many cases, it is up to the artist to choose which paper works best for the project at hand. We find certain papers have properties more suited for specific uses in our projects than others. Here we share some of our favorite papers and how we like to use them.

Lazertran Transfer Paper is used to transfer images onto nonporous surfaces. Simply print ink-jet or toner-based images directly onto the paper and then immerse the paper in water to release the decal. The decal is applied to the receiving surface.

Cardstock, sometimes referred to as cover-weight paper, is available in a variety of sizes, weights, textures and colors. We use cardstock constantly. We love it because it easily accepts paint and ink without warping and is sturdy enough to support a nicely embellished scrapbook layout. Unless otherwise noted, we use Bazzill cardstock.

Chipboard is the unsung hero of many of our memory arts projects. It is a very thin, unfinished cardboard. Use chipboard to make lightweight covers in bookmaking, to create interesting embellishments without adding bulk, and as a support for scrapbook pages with heavy or bulky page elements.

Painting Supplies

Besides basic acrylic paints, you'll need gesso and brushes for painting projects.

Gesso: A paint-like substance made from ground acrylic, gesso is used to prepare surfaces such as canvas or wood for painting. Gesso is available most often in white or black; occasionally it may be found in dark brown. White gesso may also be combined with acrylic craft paints to lighten them.

Bristle brush: Use a bristle brush to apply paint, glue or gel mediums to a variety of surfaces. These brushes come in a variety of sizes and shapes; quality varies from inexpensive synthetic to more costly natural bristles.

Bookmaking Supplies

In addition to your regular tool kit, you'll need some specialized tools to make handmade books.

Gaffer's Tape, used for bookbinding, was originally used to tape down camera/electronic equipment and electrical cords in the theatre and film industry. It's thick, durable and water-resistant, and can be embossed and written on. It is available in solid colors and in patterns.

Book Cloth is backed with paper and is used for book covers or book spines/hinges.

Transfer Mediums

For some of our projects, we transfer images from photos onto other surfaces, including fabric and tile. Transferring images is easier than it sounds—all you need is some transfer medium.

Regular Gel Medium (Matte) is an acrylic polymer that is highly effective in producing image transfers of toner or ink-jet copies onto fabric. Gel medium is also a great dimensional adhesive, as well as a glazing compound to brush over completed artwork.

Soft Gel Medium (Matte) is slightly softer than regular gel, but the properties and uses remain substantially the same. Soft gel is highly effective for ink-jet transparency image transfer projects.

Book Board, sometimes referred to as binder's board or cover board, is most frequently used for the front and back covers of handmade books. Book board is usually .08" to .09" (2mm to 2.5mm) thick. If you have a hard time locating book board, glue together a couple of pieces of chipboard as a substitute. Most book board retailers will custom cut it for you for an additional fee, which is well worth it since a standard paper trimmer can't cut through it. If you do cut book board yourself, use a heavy-duty craft knife or a utility knife.

Adhesives

Memory artists have a great variety of adhesives to choose from. You'll find our favorites here.

UHU: A pinkish-purple color that turns clear when dry is the hallmark of a UHU glue stick. Colored glue is helpful when gluing paper on a book cover, as it allows for a consistent application. UHU also comes in clear.

PVA: This glue is an archival-safe, acid-free white glue very popular with book artists. It is especially effective for gluing down thicker handmade papers.

Découpage Medium: This clear glue is used as an adhesive as well as a finish or protective coat over paper.

Diamond Glaze: A dimensional adhesive often used to adhere embellishments to memory art pieces, this glue may also be used to create a clear, glass-like finish.

Tacky Glue and **Ultra Thick Designer Tacky Glue:** Multipurpose white glue products like these are used to adhere dimensional elements, fabrics and ribbons. It is fairly inexpensive and dries clear.

E6000: This workhorse adhesive is an exceptional dimensional adhesive to use on wood, metal and glass. Because the vapors may be harmful, we recommend that this glue be used sparingly and in a well-ventilated area. Drying time for E6000 may be longer than for other adhesives, but the bond is permanent.

Perfect Paper Adhesive: Similar to PVA, PPA is available in both gloss and matte finish. It works well as a protective coating on paper, especially in matte finish.

Cutting, Poking and Smoothing Tools

When working with paper, you'll often need to smooth paper, create sharp creases or poke fine holes.

Brayer: A handheld tool with a roller, a brayer is used to roll out air bubbles and wrinkles on adhered paper surfaces. Brayers are available with interchangeable rollers for different purposes.

Bone Folder: A handheld tool with one rounded end and one pointed end, a bone folder is used to make score lines on cardstock to create a fold, or to burnish a fold line for a nice sharp crease.

Awl: A handheld tool with a sharp point, an awl is used primarily by book artists to pierce holes for stitching.

Fabric Supplies

Generally, paper tools may be used to work with fabric. You will also need a couple of specialized materials.

Printable Fabric, usually a smooth paper-backed cotton or cotton canvas, is specially prepared to run through your home printer. Although you can make your own printable fabric by cutting it and ironing (yes, we said ironing) freezer paper onto the back, we have found it easier (and sometimes less expensive) to buy it premade.

Fabric Spray Stiffener is a liquid substance sprayed on fabrics to stiffen them. We recommend spraying in a well-ventilated area and drying outdoors whenever possible. When the fabric is dry and stiff, it may be run through a die cut machine. Cotton fabrics such as quilting fabric and canvas usually work best.

Basic Tool Kit

Before you dive into the projects in this book, collect a few all-purpose tools that you'll use for almost anything you make.

Basic Tool Kit: *clockwise from left* paper cutter, scissors, metal ruler, bone folder, pencils, craft knife, self-healing cutting mat, brayer, glue stick.

Paper Arts

Do you have drawers full of ledger paper, decorative paper and cardstock? Are there shoeboxes crammed with old receipts, letters and postcards stuffed under your bed? "Why am I keeping all of this junk?" you may ask yourself during frantic bouts of spring cleaning or when attempting to stick to ambitious New Year's resolutions.

But no, perish the thought and keep the paper!

Those drawers and boxes brimming with paper can be your creative fodder. In fact, one of the things we adore about paper artistry is the literally limitless opportunities to incorporate inventive and unexpected paper elements into our projects. Our obsession with collecting all things paper began with construction paper, stationery and top-secret diaries as little girls and has grown to include things like maps, vintage stationery and office supplies.

If someone in your house grumbles that you are a packrat, we'll just keep this next part between us: Our objective in this section is to do a little paper enabling! After making some of the projects in this section, we hope you'll begin (or expand) your own stash of paper, trinkets and treasures. Most of our favorite paper supplies can be found around the house, and in any of the other places we go every day.

So yes, go ahead and keep that pretty paper bag from the trendy little gift shop. You never know when it will come in handy.

Flip-Flop Girls

HIGH SCHOOL HERE WE COME!!

SHOP TIL WE DROP   WE LOVE THE MALL

good friend

You can never have too many shoes!

kristen & alyssa

Flip-Flop Girls

According to my daughter and her girlfriend, Kristen, you can never have too many pairs of flip-flops! Take one look into my daughter's bedroom and closet to confirm this fact—be they simple and rubber-soled or fancy leather flip-flops, these functional and fashionable sandals are lined up under the edge of her dresser and heaped in piles in her closet. Flip-flops come in every color and are inexpensive, so I guess if you have to have a shoe obsession, this is the one to have!

by Tena

Make it Yours

I absolutely love using all types of cardboard on layouts. Cardboard is very easy to alter and is extremely lightweight. Experiment with inks, embossing powders or fabric dyes to give your chipboard and cardboard a facelift!

Art Supplies

baffled cardboard

colored corrugated cardboard

cardstock

patterned paper {Kangaroo and Joey}

chipboard strips, shapes, corners and bookplate {Heidi Swapp Designs}

rub-on letters {Making Memories, Autumn Leaves}

letter stickers {Deluxe Designs}

trim {Offray}

acrylic paint {Delta}

bristle brush

UHU glue stick

double-sided tape {Magic Scraps}

fine-grit sandpaper

⅛" (3mm) handheld hole punch

basic tool kit

1 • Drybrush background and accents

Use a bristle brush to drybrush white paint around the edges of the
baffled cardboard backing, chipboard flowers and a photo corner.
Allow the paint to dry. Use fine-grit sandpaper to further distress
the painted chipboard and cardboard as desired.

2 • Apply rub-ons to chipboard strips

Rub letters onto the chipboard strips to spell out names and
phrases. Also apply some flower rub-ons to a few more chipboard
strips, following the manufacturer's instructions.

3 • Adhere pictures and accents to page

Apply the glue stick to the back of the blue baffled cardboard
and adhere it to the painted chipboard background, leaving some
white paint visible around the edges. Next, adhere the pictures
to the layout. Accent the pictures with torn-out flowers and the
strips of chipboard decorated with words and images. To finish,
punch holes in the centers of the chipboard flowers using a ⅛"
(3mm) hole punch. Thread ribbon through the holes and tie them
to embellish the flower centers. Adhere the flowers to the layout
using a glue stick.

PICTURE PERFECT

*I often use photo cropping tools to
focus my photos on the story I wish
to tell on my scrapbook pages and
projects. My original photos for
this layout included much more
of the background, as well as
more of their legs in the flip-flop
photos. My layout was about their
friendship and shared obsession
with flip-flip sandals, so when
cropping the photos, I focused on
these two things and eliminated
other distracting elements.*

Forever Friends

by Carol

Art Supplies

cardstock {Basic Grey}

foam core

twill

rickrack and flower belt buckle

tar gel {Golden's}

abstract shape rubber stamps
{Stampotique, Stampington & Co.,
Hero Arts}

pink and green acrylic paint {Delta}

brown antiquing polish
{Plaid Industries}

foam paintbrush

Diamond Glaze or E-6000 adhesive

fine-grit sandpaper

basic tool kit

With their idealism and simplicity, children take things at face value, enjoying each moment as it comes without worrying about the future—something we adults couldn't do even if we tried. When I saw this photo of Mike Hannau with his childhood playmate, loaned to me by his wife, I was captivated by the obvious affection between the two children. It doesn't matter whether or not they remained friends, because at that time, in their minds, they were going to be friends forever.

1 • Cut foam core tiles

Using a craft knife with a sharp blade, cut the sheet of foam core into small tiles. Vary the size of the tiles you cut to accommodate the size of the letter or image you will stamp onto each tile.

2 • Apply tar gel to foam tile

Sand the shiny surface of a foam core tile. Apply clear tar gel to the tile with a paintbrush. Allow the tar gel to set up a bit, but do not let it harden completely.

Make it Yours

When I was making these tiles, my mind was busily thinking of other ways to use them. Immediately, I thought of using them on the front of a card to spell out "thanks" or "love." Or, cut tiles of varying sizes and colors and create a pattern as the cover of a book. How about this? Cover the sides and top of a cigar box with unfinished tiles of the same size, leaving a bit of space between them. "Grout" between the tiles with a bit of modeling paste. When the grout is dry, cover the surfaces with tar gel and then stamp your pattern into the whole surface. Paint or color wash for an Old World frescoed look.

FUN WITH FOAM

Foam core is great to use on paper layouts because it is lightweight but still dimensional. Foam is best cut with a craft knife that has a new blade that is extremely sharp. Press lightly when cutting and make several passes with the knife to avoid compressing the edges of the foam.

3 • Stamp into tar gel

When the tar gel is set up, carefully press the tile into a rubber stamp. Rubber stamps with deep impressions work best. Allow the tar gel to dry completely. Repeat steps two and three for the remaining foam tiles, using alphabet stamps to spell out the title of your page and using textured stamps for some additional squares.

4 • Paint tiles

When the tiles are dry, paint them with acrylic paints. Apply a coat of paint and then lightly wipe the paint away to create a mottled look.

5 • Apply antiquing polish

Once the paint is dry, apply antiquing polish to each of the tiles. Wipe the antiquing polish off of the raised part of the tile, and allow the polish to settle into the impressed areas to give contrast. For the tiles stamped with letters, the antiquing polish will settle into the letters themselves.

6 • Finish page

Decorate the page as you like, and adhere the letter and texture tiles to the layout with a good dimensional adhesive such as Diamond Glaze or E-6000.

Steven and Mr.Gecko

by Tena

Summer 2005

[Steven and Mr. Gecko]

Sometimes a photo can truly speak volumes! I laughed out loud when my cousin, Dana, shared this photo of her son Steven holding up the gecko lizard he caught. Steven's joy and excitement with his new acquisition is obvious in these photos. I enhanced the photos with this beautiful paper-and-cord strip that picks up the deep greens, blues and browns in the photos. The cording lends some brighter tones to the overall effect.

Make it Yours

Thicker cord options, such as hemp or decorative fabric cording, completely change the look of this technique. Feel free to play around—solid papers coated with Diamond Glaze resemble stained glass. Letters and other embellishments can also be cut from the paper-and-cord accent.

Art Supplies

cardstock

chipboard

solid-color paper and patterned paper
{K&Company, Basic Grey}

decorative or Mizuhiki cording
{Yasutomo}

textured lines rubber stamp
{Hampton Arts Stamps}

royal blue acrylic paint
{FolkArt}

foam paintbrush

die cut {CK Printers Type font from QuicKutz}

UHU glue stick

double-sided tape {Provo Craft}

basic tool kit

1 • Stamp background

Use a foam brush to apply a thin layer of blue acrylic paint to a texture stamp. Stamp the blue paint onto the solid-color paper background in three columns. Allow the paint to dry.

2 • Apply paper to chipboard strip

Cut out a piece of chipboard to a size that fits your layout (mine is 2" [5cm] wide). Cover the chipboard with double-sided tape and trim it to fit. Set the tape-covered chipboard strip aside.

Cut patterned paper in complementary colors and motifs into angled strips. Then cut the strips down to about 2½" (6cm) pieces. Stick one of the paper pieces to the chipboard strip, flush with the bottom. You'll trim the edges of the papers later.

3 • Apply cording

Cut 2½" (6cm) pieces of decorative cording. Lay one piece of decorative cording flush up against the edge of the first piece of paper.

4 • Finish chipboard strip

Continue adhering the patterned paper and the decorative cording until you cover the entire strip. Trim the paper and the cording flush with the edges of the chipboard strip.

5 • Place pictures and paper-and-cord strip

Place pictures on the stamped scrapbook paper and then mount the decorated chipboard strip on the layout with a glue stick or a tape runner. When using a glue stick, use a brayer over the paper to ensure that it adheres.

To finish the page, punch out die cut letters for the title and for any other information you want to include. Mount the page on a piece of cardstock for extra support.

Love...by Example

by Carol

Art Supplies

cardstock

solid-color paper {K&Company}

chipboard letters {Heidi Swapp}

brown and blue brads {SEI}

wooden tag {Chatterbox}

clear tags {American Tag}

twill with eyelets

ribbon

repositionable flower mask {Heidi Swapp}

rubber stamp {Postmodern Design}

brown ink {Ancient Page by Clearsnap}

light blue acrylic paint {Delta}

foam paintbrush

UHU glue stick

repositionable tape

basic tool kit

Make it Yours

Try weaving different papers together as well. Two patterned papers, one with a bold pattern and the other more subtle, create a more vibrant background. Or, weave a solid with a pattern. For a great Boho chic look, weave a paisley with a metallic, and add jewels or metallic paints.

Henry Ward Beecher, an American theologian and abolitionist, wrote, "We never know the love of a parent till we become parents ourselves." His are wise words indeed—and oh, so true. I have been blessed with parents who love their children, their grandchildren and most definitely each other. I created this layout of my parents to honor and thank them for being great examples and role models of love in action. I really liked this photo of Mom and Dad, even though I couldn't coax much of a smile out of them.

1 • Begin paper grid

To make the paper grid, cut a piece of solid-color paper that is the size you want the paper grid to be into equal-size strips. The size of the strips depends on the size of the background page and the size of the photo. In this project, the strips are ½" x 8" (1cm x 20cm). I used 13 horizontal strips and 12 vertical strips. When all the strips are cut, tape one end of each of the vertical strips to the top of a piece of cardstock with small pieces of repositionable or clear tape.

2 • Weave in horizontal strips

Start to create the woven grid by sliding one strip of paper under, over, under all of the vertical strips. When the strip is fully woven under and over all of the vertical strips, slide it to the top of the grid so that it rests against the taped border. Continue to weave the remaining horizontal strips until the paper grid is finished.

3 • Paint over flower masks

Peel the repositionable flower masks from their backing and place them on top of the paper grid. Use a foam brush to paint over the flowers with light blue acrylic paint. Apply the paint sparingly so that some areas of the paper grid remain unpainted. Allow the paint to dry and peel off the flower masks.

4 • Adhere paper grid to background paper

Prepare the background paper and lay it on your work surface. To remove the paper grid, simply flip it up from its cardstock backing so that it "hinges" on the pieces of tape. Remove the tape from the top edge of the grid and adhere it to the background paper with a glue stick. Brayer over the top of the paper grid to secure it. If you like, attach brads of different colors and sizes to the end pieces of the grid.

5 • Add photo, title and accents

Adhere a picture to the center of the paper grid with a glue stick. Use chipboard letters for the title and adhere them above the photo. As final accents, add a strip of twill with eyelets and tie on tags with wording stamped in brown ink.

Imperial Beach

by Tena

I have always loved the look of watercolor paintings of beach and ocean scenes, so I decided to paint my own watercolor backgrounds to go with the beach photos from this summer's family vacation. Painting your own background paper allows you to custom-match your paper to the colors in your photos to really pull the theme of a page or a book together. I picked colors that matched the beach clothes my children were wearing. The result is a book that has a beachy feel—even the barely-painted white background is reminiscent of foamy water.

Art Supplies

papier mâché box and accordion {Melissa Frances}

watercolor paper {Strathmore}

watercolor paints {Nicholson's}

blue elastic

powdered pigment {Perfect Pearls}

alphabet rubber stamps {Fontwerks}

archival ink {Ranger}

paint glaze {Delta}

white acrylic paint {FolkArt}

bristle brushes

glaze pen {Sakura}

PVA bookbinder's glue {Books by Hand}

double-sided tape {Tombow}

basic tool kit

Make it Yours

If watercolor paper isn't your cup of tea, consider covering a box like this by découpaging patterned paper onto it or wrapping it with patterned paper like a package. Use bits and pieces of patterned paper on the accordion book to coordinate the two.

1 • Paint book and box white

Lightly paint the mâché box and accordion with a mixture of two parts white acrylic paint to one part glaze. Allow the mixture to dry.

2 • Paint watercolor paper

Cut pieces of watercolor paper to the proper size (7½" x 7½" [19cm x 19cm] in this case) for the accordion pages of the book and for the top of the box. Dip a paintbrush in water and touch it to a small piece of Peerless paint paper to transfer the paint to your brush. Apply the paint to the watercolor paper, using your chosen colors.

3 • Stamp on letters and fill in with paint

When the paint is dry, use rubber stamps to stamp on wording for each page. Fill in the stamped letters by hand, painting them in a slightly darker shade of paint mixed with Perfect Pearls pigment to give the letters a light sparkle.

4 • Finish book and box

Adhere photos to the watercolor paper with double-sided tape. Use a glaze pen in a complementary color to write journaling on paper for the inside of the box lid.

To finish, adhere each watercolor page to the box and accordion using PVA bookbinder's glue and a paintbrush. Brayer all surfaces to ensure the watercolor paper adheres securely. Cut small strips of watercolor paper to glue to the sides of the box for additional embellishment. When the book dries, secure it closed with the blue elastic.

My Tribute to Grandpop

I spent hours in antique and fabric stores looking for buttons in the exact shade of blue to tie this design together. In the end, I decided make my own buttons out of paper clay. I suppose sometimes necessity really is the mother of invention—making my own buttons turned out to be an inexpensive way to achieve the exact look I wanted. To change the look of your project, you might use mini flower cutters and brightly colored paints.

by Carol

Make it Yours

I used these buttons to decorate the cover of a vintage record album, but they can be used in many different ways. Use one as a center for a flower, line them up on the sides of a picture frame, or add them to the corners of a photo for an interesting embellishment. Add threads, waxed linen or wire to the holes for texture and more dimension.

1. Adhere papers to album and prepare photo

Select the photo you'd like to use for the album cover and insert it into a large slide mount. Cut out different-sized squares and rectangles from scrapbook paper in complementary colors and patterns. Adhere the papers to the album cover with a glue stick. Stamp several tags with text or designs. Stamp the title of the album onto a narrow piece of solid-color paper. Begin to highlight some of the papers with brown ink to create an aged effect.

Art Supplies

vintage record album

patterned paper and solid-color paper {SEI Wild Asparagus}

small paper tags

large slide mount {Foofala}

brown eyelets

paper clay {Creative Paperclay Company}

round mini cookie cutters

rubber stamps {Ma Vinci's Reliquary, Stampotique, PSX}

brown ink {Ranger}

gesso

light blue acrylic paint {Delta}

foam paintbrush

Diamond Glaze

eyelet setter

UHU glue stick

wax paper

makeup sponge

awl

button to use as template

basic tool kit

2. Highlight album cover with brown ink

Adhere the framed picture to the album cover. Continue to highlight other areas of the album with brown ink using a makeup sponge.

PAPER CLAY

Paper clay is a soft, very pliable clay made out of paper fibers. It is easily rolled and shaped, and you can make impressions on its surface with rubber stamps or other objects. This type of clay is air dried, thus eliminating the need for a special oven to bake the clay pieces. It is non-toxic and safe for use around children and pets.

3 • Roll out paper clay for buttons

Knead a small amount of paper clay until it is soft and pliable. Lay the clay on a piece of wax paper, and use a brayer to roll the clay into a flat sheet about ⅛" (3mm) thick.

4 • Cut out clay buttons

Use a round mini cookie cutter to create the buttons. At this stage, you may also make a buckle to thread the paper with the title through. Simply cut a larger circle from the paper clay and punch out another circle in the center of the buckle. Then create a small "spoke" from paper clay and press either end into the back of the open circle. (See photo of finished album, page 26.)

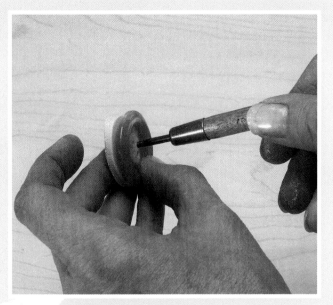

5 • Create button holes

Use an awl to punch holes in the buttons. To align button holes exactly, set a premade button on top of the clay button and poke the awl through the holes. Set the buttons aside to dry. Depending upon weather and humidity, it may take up to 24 hours for the buttons to dry completely. You may want to turn the buttons so they dry evenly.

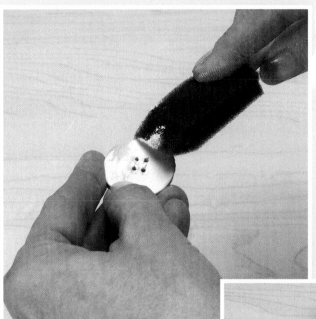

6 • Paint buttons

When the clay buttons and buckle are completely dry, paint them with acrylic paint mixed with gesso or antiquing gel. Allow the paint to dry. You can seal the clay accents with a lacquer or a product such as Diamond Glaze, both of which create a glossy look.

PAPER TASSELS

To create the funky paper tassel used inside this book, cut a strip of paper approximately 2½" x 1½" (6cm x 4cm). Use scissors to cut mini strips from the bottom to about ¼" (6mm) from the top to create a fringe. Create a string loop by tying the ends of the string in a knot. Wrap the fringed piece of paper in the shape of a cone around the knot. Apply some glue to the ends of the paper to hold it together and pinch the top of the paper over the knot. Attach the tassel to the page through an eyelet or punched hole.

7 • Finish album cover

Adhere the paper clay buttons to the photo album with Diamond Glaze. Thread the strip of paper stamped with the album title through the buckle, and adhere both the buckle and the paper to the album cover.

Generations

by Tena

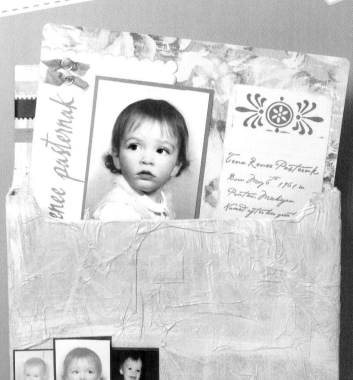

I have always enjoyed memory art projects that celebrate the similarities between generations of family members, and I'd been wanting to create a project to showcase the baby portraits I have of my mother, myself and my daughter. I found the perfect showcase for my idea when I happened upon this papier mâché portfolio while shopping online one day. When I saw it, I immediately thought it would make a great container for a series of related scrapbook layouts...the rest is literally family history!

Art Supplies

BOX TO HOLD SCRAPBOOK LAYOUTS

papier mâché portfolio {Stampington}

tissue paper

cardstock

ribbon {May Arts}

Velcro

buttons

gesso

light pink acrylic paint {Liquitex}

foam brushes

Mod Podge matte finish

tacky glue

PVA glue

basic tool kit

SCRAPBOOK LAYOUTS

patterned paper {K&Company, Wild Asparagus, Making Memories}

foam stamp {Making Memories}

archival ink

Xyron 510 and adhesive

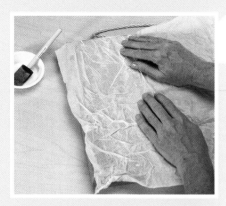

1 • Cover portfolio with tissue paper

Cut two pieces of white tissue paper to a size that is 2" (5cm) larger than the surface you will be covering. Gently crinkle the tissue paper into a ball to add wrinkles. Unfold the tissue paper and set it aside. Use a foam brush to coat one side of the portfolio with PVA glue. Adhere the tissue paper to the glue-covered surface, purposely leaving crinkles in the tissue paper. Allow the glue to dry completely. When the glue is dry, trim away the excess tissue paper, and repeat the process for the other side of the portfolio, as well as for the side panels. Allow the portfolio to dry for at least one hour before moving on to the next step.

2 • Paint tissue paper

Apply pale pink paint to the surface of the portfolio in a shabby fashion. When the pink paint is dry, apply a light coat of white gesso over the pink with a dry brush. Allow the paint to dry.

Make it Yours

Papier mâché containers come in all shapes and sizes—hatboxes, trunks, jewelry boxes, you name it. Pick a shape suited to the memorabilia collection you are housing within it to customize your project. Your local craft store is a great place to find these types of items.

3 • Apply Mod Podge matte finish

To seal and protect the wrinkled tissue surface of the portfolio, brush on a light coat of Mod Podge matte with a foam brush. Allow it to dry.

4 • Create ribbon handle

Wrap ribbons around the portfolio's flap and adhere them with tacky glue. Also adhere a piece of Velcro to the inside center of the portfolio flap and to the main part of the portfolio for a secure closure. To create a handle for the portfolio, cut a 6" to 8" (15cm to 20cm) length of sturdy ribbon and thread either end through one of the grommets in the back of the portfolio. Knot the ends of the ribbon to secure the handle.

5 • Finish portfolio

Print the title for the portfolio in mirror image on brown cardstock. I used the font Lassigue Dmato from www.myfonts.com here. Cut the letters out by hand using scissors or a craft knife. Run the hand-cut letters through a Xyron machine to apply adhesive to their backs. Apply them to the front of the portfolio.

To finish the portfolio, mat photos and apply them to the front of the portfolio to support the theme you chose.

Little Things

the best things in life are the little things. The best things in life are

LITTLE THINGS

mean alot. Little things mean alot. Little things mean a lot

by Tena

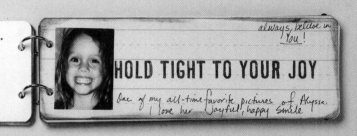

Let nothing dim the light that shines within.
Maya Angelou

the mind determines what is possible and the heart surpasses it. Pilar Coolinta

always, believe in You!

HOLD TIGHT TO YOUR JOY

One of my all-time favorite pictures of Alyssa. I love her Joyful, happy smile

Art Supplies

chipboard

blank flash cards {Spectra}

lined flash cards {Spectra}

index print photos
{printed at film processor}

hinge rings

transparencies {Apollo}

elastic book closure {7 Gypsies}

red ink {StazOn}

Pigma Micron pen {Sakura}

corner rounder

standard hole punch

UHU glue stick

basic tool kit

Sometimes it seems only certain things are "appropriate" memory art subjects: birthdays, holidays, family vacations. And sometimes it seems we "have to" use certain supplies. Well, sometimes I like to be unconventional. To create this little book, I broke all the rules. My theme is not any big event—in fact, it's the opposite. I'm celebrating the little things, since unexpected jokes, favorite photos and kisses goodnight are often truly the biggest things. I also use unconventional materials from the office supply store, like flash card blanks and transparencies printed with quotes and my family's "little things."

Make it Yours

I am definitely not in love with my own handwriting, but some sentimental projects really look best with my personal script. Since my writing isn't naturally good, I use certain tricks for making it look good. For instance, I lightly sketch my wording with a pencil to be sure the text fits. And I also practice writing with the pen I'll be using to get comfortable with the flow of ink.

1 • Create flash card pages

To make the book's pages, round the corners of the flash cards and cut pieces of chipboard to the same size. Adhere each flash card to a piece of chipboard with a glue stick. Brayer over the flash card to make sure it adheres well.

2 • Print text onto flash card pages

Use a computer word processing program to type up quotes to be printed onto the flash cards. I used the Highlights font from Autumn Leaves. You will need to change the orientation of the page to landscape to get the text to print properly. When you are happy with the positioning of the quotes on your document, print the page out and lightly tape the flash cards on top of the printed quotes. Run the sheet back through the printer. Remove the flash cards from the paper backing.

3 • Create transparency pages

Print page titles onto transparency sheets, making sure to change your printer's setting to "transparency" for the best results. Cut around the titles to make transparency pages that match the size of the flash card pages. Ink around the edges of each transparency page with brown ink by lightly pressing the edges into the ink pad.

4 • Add hand journaling and attach elastic

Write journaling by hand and attach any photos to the lined flash card pages. Paginate the book and punch two holes on the left of each page for hinge rings. Insert all of the pages onto two hinge rings. To finish the book, punch two small holes on the back page of the book to attach the elastic closure.

Family 4 Each Other

Everyone loves to open a box to see what wonderful surprises rest inside. I am no exception. Using a purchased papier mâché box that is cut, painted and altered with photos and journaling is a great way to create a three-dimensional piece of coffee table or bookshelf art. Three mini altered children's board books are housed in this box, with each book depicting characteristics about my husband, my daughter and me. Consider the possibilities...mini accordions, mini tins, pop-ups, mini card sets...endless!

by Carol

Make it Yours

A small box like this one would also work well as a new take on a travel journal. Simply decorate the inside and outside of the box with photos from your trip and coordinating papers. Add journaling to tell of your travel adventures. Then, insert a mini book with more journaling and paper ephemera collected from the journey. Tiny books like these are perfect for the tickets, receipts, maps and trinkets you've picked up during your travels.

Art Supplies

papier mâché box

patterned paper {MOD, DMD}

brass numbers

chipboard letters {Heidi Swapp, L'il Davis}

wooden dowel cap and half rounds {Lara's Crafts}

mini board books

ribbon {May Arts}

gesso

yellow, green, blue and orange acrylic paint {Making Memories}

rubber stamps {Turtle Press, L'il Davis, EK Success}

ink {Ancient Page by Clearsnap}

paintbrush

UHU glue stick

tacky glue

E6000

basic tool kit

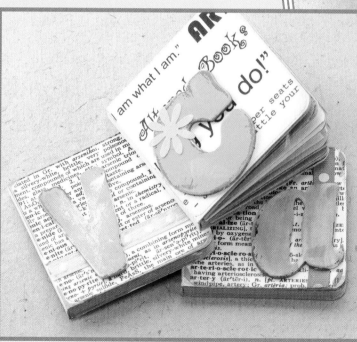

1 . Paint box and cut sides

Paint the inside and outside of a papier mâché box with white gesso. Slit the four side corners of the box with a craft knife so the sides lay flat.

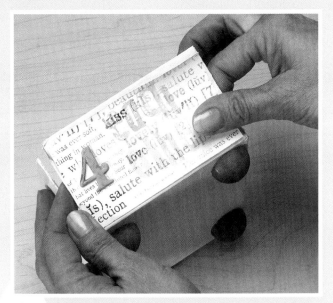

2 . Attach box "feet"

Paint four wooden half rounds orange and glue them as "feet" to each corner on the bottom of the box with tacky glue.

3 . Decorate box sides

Adhere decorative paper to each side of the box with a glue stick. My box has a family theme, so I painted a brass number to represent each family member and glued them on with E6000. Add any further embellishments that you like with paint and stamps.

4 • Decorate box top

Create a title for the box top with painted chipboard letters. Arrange them on the lid with patterned papers and a painted wooden dowel cap as a "handle."

5 • Decorate inside of box

Add photos and journaling to the insides of the box and ink the edges. To close the box, simply fold up the sides and slide on the box top to secure them in place.

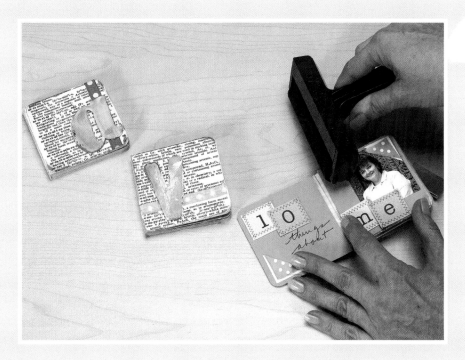

6 • Make mini books

Alter several mini board books to fit inside the box, using decorative paper, stamps and chipboard letters. Brayer any papers or photos to make sure they are well adhered.

Paper Arts Gallery

Pure

To create the title, mix two different colors of chipboard alphabets. Cut around the negative letters of one color and insert the positive letters of the other color. Sand and distress the letters and soak them in walnut ink. Dry the letters with an iron.

by Heidi Swapp

My Sister, My Friend

To celebrate the special friendship I have with my sister, I created this layout using paper tiles covered with paper and printed the central photo onto canvas photo paper. To make a spread like this one, cover a piece of chipboard with newsprint-patterned paper for the background. Then cover paper tiles with patterned paper and adhere them to the page. Print the title and other wording onto an adhesive transparency, cut them out and adhere them to the page. To finish, print a photo onto canvas photo paper and adhere it to the page with photo tape.

by Tena Sprenger

Bloom and Grow

To make a layout like this one, glue two pieces of patterned paper together with the pattern on the outside. In this layout, the pieces are 2" x 12" (5cm x 30cm). Fold the glued piece in half lengthwise. Make diagonal cuts of varying lengths along the folded edge of the paper. Unfold it and lay it flat. Starting at one end, fold up the second V and crease. Repeat with every other V, folding up and creasing until you reach the end. Lift up the first V that is pointing down and tuck it under the V pointing up. Continue this process all the way to the end of the paper.

The result? A fabulous braided-paper look that may be used as an accent across a page or folded over the top or bottom of a page.

by Miley Johnson

Your Future

I loved the look of my son in this photo and thought this layout would be a perfect way to share my thoughts about some of the things he has in store in the years to come. I liked the idea of revealing the words behind the softly painted papers, making the idea of the future seem less concrete and more dreamy.

To make a page like this one, use masking fluid to journal words onto a cardstock background. Lightly paint over the entire page with white acrylic paint. When the mask is dry, peel it off. Type up some journaling and print it directly onto painted areas. Add a photo and create circles with Twinkling H2Os and brads. Handwrite the title with masking fluid, paint it and then peel off the masking fluid when it has dried.

by Jessie Baldwin

Parisian Reflections

Using a piece of glass as a background is an easy way to add a layer of elegance to a paper arts project. To make a piece like this one, first follow the manufacturer's directions to adhere a Lazertran image transfer to a piece of cut glass. For the background of the transferred image, adhere paper with a script design to the back of the glass with Diamond Glaze. A simple design works best as the background for a transfer image—anything too complicated will compete with the photo image.

by Kelly Anderson

Simply You

To make your own tribute to a loved one, carefully cover cut-out paper accents with tissue paper, using découpage medium to adhere the tissue. After the tissue dries, rub the shapes with gold Rub 'n Buff and cover the surfaces with Diamond Glaze to seal them.

by Katherine Brooks

Family Photo Boxes

I am always saving every interesting container that most people would discard, so I had accumulated a tall stack of brie cheese boxes when it dawned on me that the sides of the little boxes are almost the exact width of one of my favorite products—printed gaffer's tape! I used these cute little altered boxes to hold mini photo albums for each member of my family. You could use them as a personalized paperweight, or to hold the doodads on your desk top!

Use the empty brie cheese box to create a template to cut the paper needed to cover the top and bottom of the boxes.

by Tena Sprenger

Mother and Daughter Bridesmaids

It isn't every day that a mother and daughter share a role like this one. To commemorate the experience, I created this layout. To create the tar gel accent flowers, use an embossing tool to trace the flower image onto a metal sheet and cut it out. To decorate the flower, mix tar gel with acrylic paint according to the manufacturer's instructions. Drip tar gel across the metal to create a web-like effect. Attach a gem to form the flower center.

by Pam Kopka

Remembering to Laugh

To make the letters on a page like this one, roll out paper clay to your desired thickness. For the monogram letter, place a pre-cut chipboard letter on top of the clay and cut around it with a craft knife. Remove the chip letter, lightly stamp the clay with a foam stamp, and let the clay dry. Once fully dry, use paints and gold glaze to cover the letter. Seal the paint with découpage medium. To create letter tiles, stamp paper clay with foam stamps and cut the clay into rectangles. After the tiles are dry, use paint, antiquing medium and rub-ons to decorate.

by Katherine Brooks

by Carol Wingert

The Road Trip of a Lifetime

For a number of years now, I have been collecting unique tags from garments, food items and household goods. The graphics and various shapes are fascinating to me and the means of attachment on special tags is usually quite clever. That collection of tags inspired me to create a tag book hung on a large pin; a kilt/skirt or saddle blanket pin would also work but would have a slightly smaller profile. I created tags out of various papers—chipboard, corrugated cardstock, cardboard and mat board—and also incorporated purchased tags. Add in a slide mount, a large chipboard monogram and a flash card, and you have a fascinating assortment of hanging surfaces onto which to place your photos and journaling.

Memories of Rome

To create this simple project, I used an existing image as the background and filled it in. The background for this layout is a page from the book *Curiousa*, which depicts a photo of an old printer's box. I simply "filled" each compartment of the box with little pieces of travel ephemera from my trip to Rome.

by Kelly Anderson

Dear Nana and Papa!
We are having an amazing time at the beach. Something bout waking up to the sound of the ocean is unbelievably calming. Our days have been filled with boogie-boarding, long walks and lots of sand. Alyssa and Michael have beautiful golden beach tans, they play all day and fall asleep in an instant at night. Mike and I do not want to return to reality. See ya when we get back, lots of photos to scrapbook when I come home. Love, Tena

TO: Nana and Papa
5434 Hackamore Circle
Mesa, Arizona 85205

POST◦CA

Cant believe we are finally at the beach house for our week of rest and relaxation. Thanks so much for watching the dog we will bring you back a special treat for all your help. Today was all about building the biggest sandcastle ever... and we succeeded until the tide came in and washed it away!

see ya soon. Your

TO: Aunt Trish
56 Brown Road
Mesa, Arizona 85213

Fabric Arts

For Tena and me, textiles have long been a rich part of our creative lives. We have fond childhood memories of visits to fabric stores, running our hands along the bolts and bolts of fabric in candy colors and luscious textures. From making doll clothes, we graduated to making our own clothes, and now we incorporate fabric and notions into our memory art projects.

While we know that most of our readers enjoy the wonderful fabric textures and the variety textiles add to a piece of art, we also know that many do not sew and do not want to learn to sew. Our goal in this section is to incorporate fabrics into our projects easily by gluing them and occasionally hand-sewing them. Of course, there always has to be an "over the top" project for those looking for the ultimate challenge, so there is one project with lots of sewing.

We hope that the fabric scraps, bits of ribbon, twill and lace, printed fabrics and the image transfer techniques we use will inspire you to dig into your scrap bin, notions tin and button jar for that special something to make your project totally unique.

Family

Mom with Claudia, Lucy & Terry

by Carol

Letters and shapes made with die cuts are extremely versatile—they can be painted, crumpled, chalked and stamped, just to name a few altering techniques. When I came across fabric stiffening spray, my first thought was, "Can the stiffened fabric be used like paper in a die cut machine?" The answer is a resounding "YES!" and the result is another artistic way to use die cuts. This project, featuring my mom, her two nieces and her nephew, uses layers of fabrics, ribbons and trims. The title and flowers are die-cut fabrics.

Art Supplies

fabric in complementary colors and patterns {Moda}

ribbon {Offray}

rickrack

ink-jet printable cotton {Jacquard}

embroidery floss {DMC}

fabric stiffening spray {Beacon}

foam adhesive squares

die cuts {Ellison}

sewing needle

UHU glue stick

basic tool kit

Make it Yours

I got so excited about die cutting stiffened fabric that I immediately incorporated an idea into one of the projects I was teaching in a class. I die cut a piece of luggage out of stiffened black canvas, then lightly touched up the surface of the canvas with brown paint to create a distressed leather look. I added thin ribbons and some metal studs to recreate the look of a piece of vintage luggage. You may be surprised at how many of the old dies can be put to use again with this technique.

1 • Stiffen fabric

To prepare the fabric for die cutting, spray the fabric with fabric stiffening spray per the manufacturer's instructions. Spray in a well-ventilated area, or outdoors. When the fabric has dried and is stiff, it is ready to die cut.

2 • Cut out letters and flowers

Cut shapes and letters in the same fashion as you would cut paper. Poorly cut shapes may be the result of not enough stiffener or die cut machines that are not working properly. If making the layered flower in this project, be sure to cut out several flowers from different fabrics to layer.

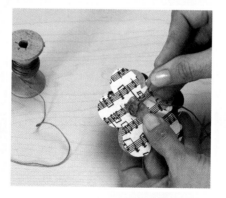

3 • Create flower letter

When creating your lettered title, place a flower under one of the letters and adhere it with foam adhesive squares to "pop" that letter and flower.

4 • Create layered flower

To create the dimensional fabric flower, layer several flower shapes cut from different fabrics. Use embroidery floss to create a looped stitch in the center of the flower to give dimension to the center of the flower and to the layout.

5 • Finish layout

Print your photo on printable fabric and adhere it to the layout with a glue stick, along with various fabrics, ribbons, laces and rickrack.

I LOVE...

I LOVE......
by Tena

THE CRAZY THINGS I FIND IN YOUR *pockets*

Your AMAZING VOCABULARY

THAT DAD IS YOUR *best* FRIEND

YOUR *passion* FOR READING

HOW YOU *talk* TO THE DOG

WHEN YOU *snuggle* UP

WATCHING STAR WARS WITH *you*

WHEN *you* WINK YOUR EYE *at* ME

YOUR *Daily* HUGS AND KISSES

THE LITTLE *freckles* ON YOUR NOSE

One of my favorite places to look for inspiration is in the pages of my favorite magazines. I came across a really eye-catching vertical list of numbers in an advertisement for a shopping list, and I clipped out the page and filed it to use as a layout idea for one of my scrapbook pages. When I started working on this page about the things I love about my son Michael, I remembered the advertisement I had clipped and filed away, and pulled it out to use as a model while designing the layout.

Art Supplies

cardboard backing

canvas fabric and patterned fabrics

cotton batting

red and white thread {Coates and Clark}

iron-on transfers {Avery}

fabric stiffener {Beacon}

clear packing tape

iron

needle

basic tool kit

Make it Yours

I really enjoy using fabrics in paper arts projects because they provide dimension and artistic variety. Next time you use canvas for a scrapbooking layout, experiment with creating your own patterned background using fabric paints and dyes, or embellish with fabrics, trims, fibers and other sewing notions.

1. Iron on text and photo

Cut a 14" x 14" (36cm x 36cm) square of natural-colored canvas and press it flat. Print a photo and text (I used AL Playbill and AL Highlights from Autumn Leaves 2004) onto iron-on transfer paper, using the suggested printer settings. Follow the manufacturer's instructions to apply the iron-ons to the canvas.

IRON ON

Be sure to use fabrics with a very smooth surface when ironing on photos. A heavily textured surface distorts photos. It is also important to use a firm surface to iron on top of—an ironing board is not firm enough. Most manufacturers recommend a wood or tile surface. Before ironing, print your iron-on elements on printer paper and arrange them on your project to be sure you are happy with design placement. (Once heat is applied to the iron-on it is no longer repositionable.)

2. Create template and cut out numbers

Hand-draw numbers to create a template for cutting numbers out of fabric. Cut out each individual number.

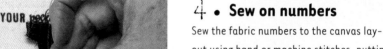

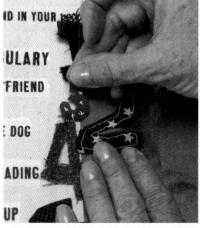

3. Trace and cut out fabric numbers

Use the template to cut out numbers one through ten, cutting each number out of a different fabric. Trace the numbers onto the backs of the fabrics, making sure to lay the numbers down backwards so that they will come out facing the right direction when cut out. Lightly spray the fabric numbers with fabric stiffener to lessen fraying.

4. Sew on numbers

Sew the fabric numbers to the canvas layout using hand or machine stitches, putting cotton batting behind some numbers to add dimension.

5. Finish layout

Stretch the edges of the canvas around the sides of the cardboard backing and secure them with clear packing tape.

Summer Memories

When I was a little girl, I loved to get postcards from friends and families we knew who were away on vacation. It always seemed to me that any place wonderful enough to have its own postcard must be a fabulous place to go on holiday! When deciding how to scrapbook these photos of our children on a summer beach vacation, postcard-style journaling seemed just the right way to commemorate how special our annual beach vacation in California truly is.

by Tena

Make it Yours

Experiment with printing scrapbook page elements you would normally print onto cardstock onto different types of printable fabrics, like photo canvas or printable silk, to give your projects a softer, shabby or sometimes vintage look.

Art Supplies

12" x 12" (30cm x 30cm)
piece of thin cardboard for mounting

cardstock

tropical fabric
{Village Screen Prints}

canvas printer fabric {Jacquard}

twine

mother-of-pearl embellishments
{7 Gypsies}

postcard stamp
{River City Rubber Works}

postmark stamp {Hero Arts}

ink {Ranger}

fabric color wash {7 Gypsies}

paintbrushes

clear packing tape {Scotch}

tacky glue

E6000 adhesive

basic tool kit

1. Cover cardboard with fabric

Stretch the fabric around the 12" x 12" (30cm x 30cm) piece of cardboard and secure the fabric to the back of the cardboard with clear packing tape.

2. Create fabric postcards

Print journaling and photos onto canvas printer fabric using an ink-jet printer. I used the font CSS Hand from Microsoft Word 2003. Stamp a postcard stamp on top of the printed journaling to create the look of a postcard.

To create an aged effect, color the edges of the fabric postcards and the photo with fabric color wash, using a small paintbrush.

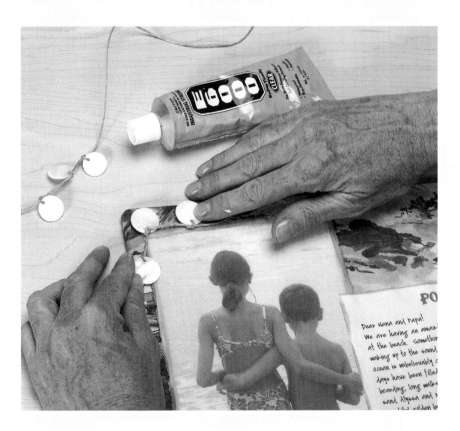

3. Add mother-of-pearl and twine accents

Adhere the postcards and the photo to the layout using tacky glue and a brayer. Cut out flowers from the fabric to add as accents, and adhere them with tacky glue. String mother-of-pearl accents onto twine and tie them in place. Use E6000 to adhere the twine and mother-of-pearl accents to the layout, taping the ends of the twine to the back of the layout to secure them.

Yes, You Are a Princess

by Tena

I love making themed mini books to celebrate the events and personalities in my life—and boy-oh-boy is my 15-year-old daughter a personality to celebrate. To start this project, I sketched out a black book with a patent leather sheen covered with pink fishnets and picked out some princess-inspired photos. Next I collected embellishments, fabrics, papers and other feminine doodads. After I found a sturdy album to support the trims and fabrics, I sat down to create. I simply picked the supplies that best supported my original vision for the book...which is fit for a princess, if I say so myself.

Art Supplies

book structure {7 Gypsies}

handmade papers {Provo Craft}

cardstock {Bazzill}

shiny black fabric {Michael Miller Memories, Michael Levine}

rhinestones and rhinestone accents

pink fishnets {Hue Stockings}

mini clipboard {Provo Craft}

bendable embossing metal

coin envelopes {Waste Not Paper}

silver mesh {Robin's Nest}

acrylic paint {Folk Art}

paintbrushes

foam paintbrush

clear packing tape

UHU glue stick

fabric glue {Duncan}

E6000 adhesive

tacky glue

basic tool kit

Make it Yours

No matter the memory topic, it's fair game for a mini book theme! When I find a topic for a book, I start collecting the elements, journaling and memorabilia pieces I want to incorporate all into one bag or box. When I start my project I have everything I need all in one place.

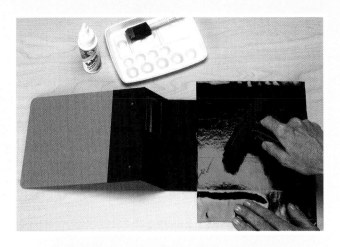

1. Cover book with shiny black fabric

Cut two pieces of black shiny fabric to a size that covers the front and back of the book, plus a 1" (3cm) border on three sides. Use a disposable paintbrush to paint tacky glue onto the surface of the book to be covered, and brayer the fabric to secure it to the cover.

2. Secure edges of paper

Turn the book face up and fold in the edges of the black fabric, tapering the corners as when wrapping a gift. Tape down the fabric with clear packing tape.

3. Cover with fishnets and add end paper

Stretch the fabric (in this case very stretchy hot pink fishnet stockings) over the front cover of the book, allowing the waistband to butt up against the border of the black paper. Secure the borders of the fishnet stockings to the inside cover of the book with clear packing tape. Cut a square of decorative paper to create an end paper for the front cover and adhere it over the fabric with fabric glue. Roll over the paper with a brayer to ensure adhesion.

4. Add aluminum corners

Cut two small squares of bendable embossing metal with strong scissors. Bend the top two corners of each square in toward each other and down to create triangles. Slip the triangles onto the corners of the book and secure them with tacky glue. Adhere pink rhinestones to the metal corners with glue. Glue on any additional trims or photos to finish the cover. To create the title, type it out in a word processing program. In this project, I used the AL Meaningful font by Autumn Leaves. Print out the title in mirror image onto the back of the paper you choose. Use a craft knife or sharp scissors to cut out the letters. Glue the letters to the cover using tacky glue.

5. Create embellishments and finish book

Create embellishments, such as the mini pink clipboard pictured above, to decorate the inside pages. To create the inside pages, cut cardstock to size after measuring the book and binder hole placement. Decorate pages with photos, fabric and/or trims to complete the book theme.

My Ancestry: the Children

by Carol

When my paternal grandfather passed away, my dad received a box full of wonderful old photos of family members as children. Many of the pictures were unlabeled, and we couldn't figure out who some of the children were. Seeing such a treasure chest of the children who were all part of my heritage in some way or another, I promptly borrowed the pictures. I wanted to make a soft, touchable and durable book to feature these beautiful children. I hinged the fabric "pages" together with twill and folded them up accordion style to make the book. The sometimes faded black-and-white pictures really stand out against the rich colors and textures of the fabric.

Art Supplies

fabric {Moda}

printable cotton {Jacquard}

quilt batting

ink-jet transparencies

assorted ribbon, lace, twill, buttons, beaded tassel

large button {Bazzill}

printed twill {Making Memories}

flower {Prima}

assorted rickrack

rubber stamps {Missing Link}

ink {Crafter's by Color Box}

soft gel medium (matte)

regular gel medium (matte)

foam paintbrush

straight pins

sewing machine

tacky glue

basic tool kit

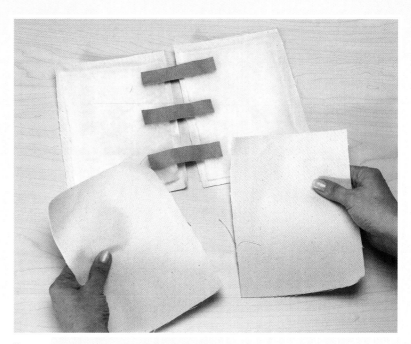

1 • Begin to make fabric pages

Cut 6" x 8" (15cm x 20cm) canvas pages and 5" x 7" (13cm x 18cm) pieces of quilt batting. Cut two pieces of canvas and one piece of quilt batting for each page. Cut hinge pieces out of torn or sewn fabric, twill or ribbon. You will need three 3" (8cm) hinge pieces for every two pages. To create the first two hinged pages, layer the pieces as follows: canvas, quilt batting, hinges, canvas.

2 • Finish hinged pages

Pin the layers in place and sew around the edges, leaving a ½" (1cm) seam. Connect another page by adding hinges on the right side of the second page. After sewing each page, remove the pins. Continue to add panels until the desired length of the book is achieved. Do not add hinges to the last panel. You may leave the edges of the pages frayed, or stitch around them.

3 • Begin gel medium transfer

Make a color or a black-and-white copy of a photo with a toner-based copier. (Ink-jet copies will produce a much lighter image.) Cut a piece of cotton canvas a bit larger than the photo to be transferred. Apply a layer of regular gel medium (matte) to the surface of the canvas with a foam brush. Be careful not to lay the medium on too thick.

4 • Transfer photo to fabric

Lay the photocopy, face down, on the gel-covered fabric. Burnish the paper with a spoon or the rounded end of a bone folder. Set the image aside to dry, preferably overnight.

5 • Moisten transferred image

When the transfer has dried, apply water to the paper and fabric with a damp sponge. You may also lay the transfer in a shallow dish of water, as shown.

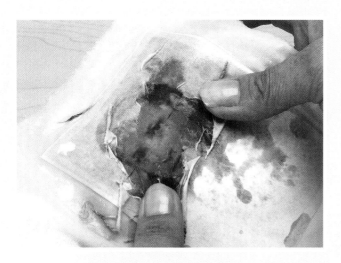

6 • Remove photocopy from fabric

As the surface of the fabric becomes moist, begin to gently rub off the paper. If necessary, dampen the transfer further and continue to rub off the paper. Continue this process until all of the paper has been removed and the image is clearly visible. This is a bit of a slow process; you don't want to rush it or apply too much moisture too quickly or the image will be lifted with the gel. Allow the transferred image to dry before adding it to your memory art project.

7 • Begin ink-jet transparency transfer

Copy a photo onto an ink-jet transparency. Apply a layer of soft gel medium to the fabric you will be using. (Smooth cotton fabrics seem to work best for this type of transfer.) Make sure the entire surface is covered with soft gel medium and that the gel is spread evenly. Lay the transparency face down into the gel and burnish well with a spoon or bone folder. Carefully lift a corner of the transparency to check the progress of the transfer. If the image is light, continue to burnish until the image transfers completely.

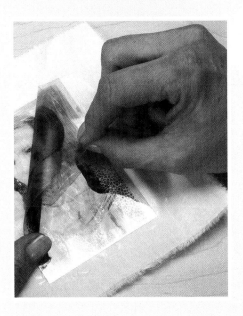

8 . Finish ink-jet transparency transfer

Slowly and gently peel away the transparency to reveal the transferred image.

9 . Create other transfers

To make a crisp, clean image, you can print your photo directly onto fabric. Simply choose a fabric with a paper "carrier" for ease in running through your printer. The image shown at far left is an example of a picture printed directly onto fabric. The images in the center (top and bottom) are gel medium transfers. The image at right is an ink-jet transparency transfer.

10 . Finish book

Glue the image transfers onto the pages of your fabric book with diluted tacky glue and add ribbon, rickrack, buttons and other kinds of accents. I also made some fabric pockets and inserted image transfers like these pull-out photos inside.

Fabric Arts Gallery

Just Friends Having Fun

These pictures of my cousin's daughter, Krystal, and her friend, Kaitlin, inspired me to create a layout depicting the innocence of these 13-year-olds in contrast to their vamping for the camera. The fabrics are girlie, lacy and soft, with the accent flowers made out of shiny, clear vinyl stamped with rubber stamps and acrylic paint.

by Carol Wingert

KAITLIN & KRYSTAL

JUST FRIENDS HAVING FUN!

by Pam Kopka

Enjoying Life

To create a multicolored fabric photo transfer like the one on this page, cut fabric pieces into strips. (Lighter fabrics work best.) Print your image on transparent iron-on transfer paper. Arrange the fabrics in the correct order on your layout. Iron on the transfer over the fabric according to the manufacturer's directions, and you have quickly created a beautiful effect.

Life has been getting a little heavy lately. Pressure is all around me. Trying to be everything is impossible. I just can't. It is time to ease up on myself and begin enjoying life again before the DAYS fly by and my children are grown.

August 20

by Jessie Baldwin

Tied

I made this page to commemorate the first day that my daughter dressed herself completely. Of course, I didn't have the heart to tell Violet that her shoes weren't tied correctly. It took quite some time to get those knots out, and actually, a couple of them still remain on the individual laces! I decided to make this page with braided paper strips that recreate the look of my daughter's shoelaces. I made ribbon strips out of fabric paper, which I really like because it tears straight and doesn't fray beyond the initial tear. I then folded the fabric paper strips together and used them as a border.

Smile Like You Mean It

To create a layout like this one, first make little chipboard shapes for the iron-on letters. Simply cut random shapes, paint them and let them dry. Then iron on the letters and rough up the edges of the shapes with some sandpaper. The flower embellishment is cut out of paper and overlapped before it is placed under the photo. The designer photo corners were just the right touch for attaching the photo to the layout.

by Heidi Swapp

Book Arts

As children, Carol and I both made our very first handmade books using paper scavenged from composition notebooks held together with simple staples. Even though we were using humble materials, we found something amazingly gratifying about constructing books and filling them with our thoughts, drawings and photos. Of course, we aren't the first to jot down the events and thoughts of our day-to-day lives. Journals, diaries, sketch books and art journals have long been kept by people from all walks of life, including great men like Benjamin Franklin and unknowns like Anne Frank. Books made by hand can serve any purpose you'd like. They can be whimsical or more serious, cohesive in theme or totally random.

We have tried to keep our bookmaking fun and have steered away from dry, technical terms that often characterize book arts. Any technical instructions we did incorporate are included because they make the process less frustrating, and also because knowing them will help you produce a well-made, professional-looking book. Technicalities aside, we have also incorporated some unexpected elements, such as metal, playing cards, transparencies, office supplies and boxes, into our books.

Our challenge to you is this: Look for unique objects with which to create. Have fun making a one-of-a-kind book you'll be proud to display and that everyone will want to look at and touch, over and over again.

100% You

by Carol

This photo of my friend's grand-daughter, Delanie, illustrates her personality so well that I didn't want to use any other pictures on the layout to detract from it. However, of course there were other pictures that fit the theme of the page that I wanted to include. To have the best of both worlds, I used the extra pictures in a mini book included in the layout. Mini books like the one here are an especially fun and interactive way to chronicle an event and to maximize space.

Art Supplies

patterned paper {Basic Grey}

cardstock

mini fabric tote bag

chipboard letters {Magistical Memories}

chipboard strips {Heidi Swapp}

wired chenille

embroidery floss

buttons

bits of leather

rubber stamps {Wendi Speciale Designs, Fontwerks}

ink {Color Box Chalk}

acrylic paint {Delta}

needle

UHU glue stick

tacky glue

basic tool kit

1 • Create fabric pouch

Cut the twill handles off a mini fabric tote bag.

2 • Stitch on paper

Cut a small piece of scrapbook paper that coordinates with the colors you are using in your layout. Thread a large needle with embroidery floss and tie a knot in the end of the floss. Stitch along the two long edges of the piece of paper in long, chunky stitches. Decorate the pouch further with text and/or other embellishments. Set the pouch aside.

3 • Begin making pages

Create a mini four-panel accordion book to insert into the bag. Cut a 4¾" x 12" (12cm x 30cm) cardstock strip. Measure and mark at 3" (8cm) intervals along the 12" (30cm) side. Score the cardstock at each mark, using either a bone folder or the scoring blade on a paper cutter.

4 • Fold paper into pages

Fold the scored paper to create a four-panel accordion. Burnish each fold with a bone folder. Embellish the mini book to coordinate with the layout.

5 • Adhere pouch

Use tacky glue to adhere the decorated pouch to the layout so that the opening is on the right side.

6 • Finish layout

Insert the finished book into the pouch to finish the layout.

Organized Chaos

by Tena

Anyone who has been into my art room at home would probably simply call it Chaos! Even though I always have piles of paper and supplies stacked around me and a crazy-messy work table, I actually do know where most things are and find a way to be creative in spite of—or perhaps because of—the disorganization usually around me.

To create a book like this, just dump the contents of your desk drawers onto your desk and you've hit the jackpot. Dig through the stuff you use every day to find unique and unusual materials to construct a handmade book about your life.

Make it Yours

If—lucky you—your workspace happens to be as neat as a pin, you can still make a clipboard book. Just make it to reflect your well-ordered nature. You might incorporate graph paper into your cover, or add neatly printed tabs to the different sections of the book so it's easily navigable.

Art Supplies

clipboard {Saunders Corp}

5" x 7" (13cm x 18cm) clasp envelopes with metal prong fasteners

cardstock

shipping tags, jewelry tags, index tags {Avery}

metal-rimmed circle tags {American Tag}

plastic photo sleeve {C-line}

tri-fold file folder {Paper Reflections}

paint chip strip {Daisy-D's}

assorted paint chip cards

clip, mailing labels

self-adhesive transparencies {Grafix}

due date slip {Silver Crow}

lined paper

report card envelope {Knock Knock}

note lists {Franklin Covey}

CD envelope

vintage labels, vintage sticker {Cavallini papers}

paper clips

twill ribbon

acrylic paint {Plaid, DecoArt, Making Memories}

foam stamps {Heidi Swapp}

rubber stamps {Stampington, Stampers Anonymous, Hero Arts}

paint glaze {Delta Sheer Color Finish}

ink {Crafter's Pigment Ink}

label maker {Dymo}

paintbrushes

basic tool kit

1 • Gather office supplies

Go to the office supply store or rummage through your desk to find some basic office supplies to use for your book. I used manila envelopes, a clipboard, tri-fold file folders, tags with string ties and paper clips to create the basic structure of my book.

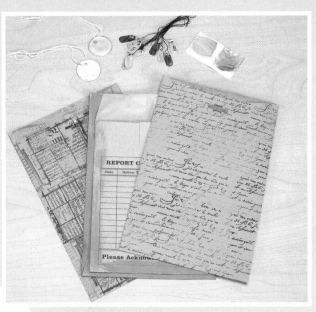

2 • Alter basic supplies with paint and stamps

Score all envelopes 1" (3cm) from the bottom so that they will flip up easily when they become your pages. Decide on a color palette and alter all of the supplies you gathered by painting them with acrylic paints and stamping text and images onto them.

3 • Paint and stamp "cover" page

Mix two parts glaze to one part paint and drybrush the mixture onto the cover page in a shabby fashion. Lightly brush darker paint onto a foam stamp and stamp on top of the "shabby" painted cover.

OFFICE SPACE

Try using these other common household supplies when making books:

- *Wrapping paper scraps*
- *Old stationery and card envelopes*
- *Fabric scraps*
- *Wallpaper scraps*
- *Leftover cardboard and chipboard*

4 • Embellish tri-fold file folder with foam stamp

To decorate with a foam stamp, simply brush paint onto the stamp with a foam brush and push it firmly down onto the paper. Stamp all over the tri-fold file folder.

5 • Construct book and add pull-out elements

Assemble all of your altered pages so that they are secured at the top by the metal clip of the clipboard. Add pull-out journaling elements to slip inside of the envelopes.

6 • Add printed journaling

Print out more journaling from your computer onto transparency pages with adhesive backing. The font I used here is Leisly from Microsoft Word. Simply peel away the transparency from the backing and adhere it to one of your embellished pages.

Family Deck

by Tena

A favorite activity in my family has always been playing games—board games, card games, computer games...you name it, we play it! We have an entire closet in our home designated for board games and card games. When I came across this oversized deck of cards, it immediately struck me as a funky way to house and create a decorative family album to showcase the members of our family...even our pets!

Art Supplies

large deck of cards {Bicycle}

miniature cards {7 Gypsies}

patterned paper {7 Gypsies}

hinged rings for binding

ribbon {May Arts, Offray, Midori}

rub-on alphabets and text {Geneva, Making Memories, 7 Gypsies)

printed gaffer's tape {7 Gypsies}

sandpaper

ink {Stampin' Up, Ranger}

makeup sponge

standard hole punch

UHU glue stick

basic tool kit

1 • Sand card box

Sand the front and back of the card box to remove the shiny surface and to prepare it to absorb ink. Apply the ink to the box with a makeup sponge to further create a distressed look.

2 • Apply decorative papers and gaffer's tape

Tear strips of decorative papers and apply them to the box using a glue stick. Brayer over the paper to secure it. Cover the "spine" of the box with printed gaffer's tape.

3 • Apply rub-on letters to miniature cards

Glue several miniature cards together in a staggered fashion. Rub on black letters to spell out "Deck." Adhere the word to the front of the card case. Apply additional words to the cover, using rub-on letters to create the title.

4 • Distress playing cards

Distress playing cards with sandpaper. To finish the distressed look, apply ink to the cards with a makeup sponge.

5 • Finish book

Punch holes in each of the playing cards and decorate them as you like. Insert hinged rings through the holes in the card pages to bind the book together. Embellish the rings with twill and ribbon.

This and That

by Tena

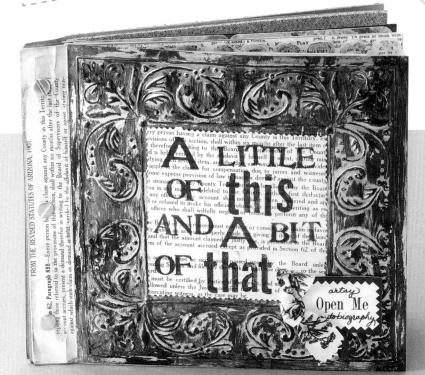

When I was gathering materials to make this book, I was looking at the world through a (slightly quirky) bookmaker's lens. Suddenly, everything looked like a book page. A plastic placemat and a tin picture frame? Perfect. Who says all your pages have to match? Choose lots of different kinds of pages to reflect your personality. My theme for this book is "artsy autobiography," and the pages are meant to convey little bits and pieces of my life and personality. You might also consider using other materials, such as canvas, fabric, wood or metal mesh.

Make it Yours

When making my "This and That" book I had so many other types of page materials I wanted to incorporate into the book...but I ran out of room!
Other materials that would be fun to utilize in a book like this would be wood, metal mesh, fabrics or wallpaper...get crazy!

Art Supplies

chipboard

corrugated cardboard

metal embossed tile
{Artistic Expressions}

plastic placemat

cork sheet

screw posts {Lineco}

postcards, open-me tag
{Chronicle Books}

patterned paper {Provo Craft, Making
Memories, 7 Gypsies}

ribbon {May Arts}

plastic slide sleeve {C-line}

vintage labels, vintage sticker
{Cavallini papers}

metal mini frame {Nunn Designs}

vintage ledger paper

glaze pens {Sakura}

rubber stamps {Postmodern Design,
Cavallini Papers, Hero Arts,
Magnetic Poetry}

foam stamp {Making Memories}

ink {Archival Ink by Ranger}

acrylic paint
{Folk Art, Making Memories}

rub 'n buff wax finish {Amaco}

soft cloth

alcohol inks {Tim Holtz, Ranger}

felt squares

varnish sealer {Delta}

sandpaper

paintbrushes

hole punch

label maker {Dymo}

tacky glue {Aleene's}

UHU glue stick

epoxy adhesive {E6000}

basic tool kit

1. Create book pages

Use a heavy-weight trimmer or craft knife to cut the desired number of pages from chipboard to a size that works for your book. My pages are 9" x 8" (23cm x 20cm). Use a bone folder to score each page 1" (3cm) from the front left side. Punch three holes to the left of the scored line, at 1" (3cm) from the top, 4" (10cm) from the top and 7" (18cm) from the top.

2. Paint metal tile for cover

Sand the embossed metal tile lightly with sandpaper and brush off any sanding dust. Lightly paint the tile with red acrylic paint. Allow it to dry. Lightly sand away some of the red paint. Apply red Rub 'n Buff wax finish with a soft cloth and buff to a sheen once it has dried. Seal the paint on the tile with a coat of clear varnish.

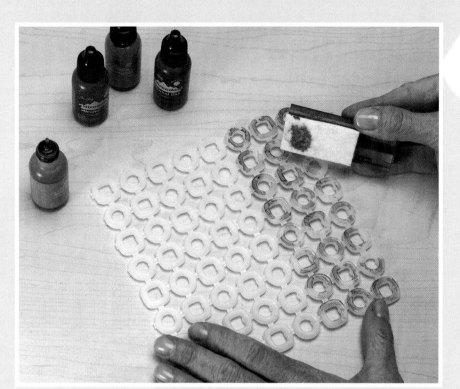

3 • Alter plastic placemat

Cut the plastic placemat to 8" x 8" (20cm x 20cm) with strong scissors or a craft knife. Squeeze alcohol ink onto a felt square and dab the ink (or inks) onto the placemat until the desired color is achieved. Mount the placemat on top of patterned text paper with tacky glue.

SHUT THE BOOK

When making a multi-material book like this, be sure to take into consideration the thickness of your pages. A combination of thick and thin pages is prefer-able to avoid making the book so thick that it can't be closed and always yawns open.

4 • Create cork page

Use tacky glue to adhere an 8" x 8" (20cm x 20cm) piece of cork to a chipboard page and brayer it for good adhesion. Use foam stamps and acrylic paint to stamp images, words and journaling as desired onto the cork.

5 • Assemble book

Paginate the book as desired, lining up the previously punched holes. Separate the screw posts, insert the top of each post through the holes in the pages and screw on the back of each screw at the back side of the book.

Ideas for Other Pages

Plastic Slide Holder Page

Cut down a plastic slide sleeve to book page dimensions and fill it with 2" x 2" (5cm x 5cm) photos. Cover the background page with patterned paper and stamp a title on the edges. Adhere the slide page to the covered chipboard page with a glue stick.

Corrugated Cardboard Back Cover

Use a razor blade and hand tearing to distress the surface of a piece of corrugated cardboard. Apply a glue stick to a piece of patterned paper and brayer it into place on the cardboard. Paint a vertical border on one side of the back cover with acrylic paint. When the paint has dried, hand-write journaling onto the page with a glaze pen.

She's Got Hatitude!

by Carol

Make it Yours

A book in a box is just plain fun. Get creative about your boxes and the types of books you put inside. How about round heavy paper coasters in a round box, or square pieces of chipboard tied together in a square box? The possibilities are bound only by your imagination.

As I was looking through photos of Ashley's early childhood, it struck me that this daughter of mine just loved hats as a little girl. She wasn't picky, either—any hat would do. She wore my hats, her dad's hats, her pop-pop's and, in a few (very few) instances, one of her own! A wooden box with a slider top that had been waiting for a project makes a great case for a fold-out accordion book. An accordion with pages of the same size did not easily fit inside the box, so I made a book with pages that increased in size from front to back.

Art Supplies

wooden box {Walnut Hollow}

patterned paper {K&Company, Iota}

chipboard letters {Magistical Memories}

buttons {SEI}

rickrack

mini flowers {Savvy Stamps}

vinyl letters {Heidi Swapp}

ribbon {Maya Road}

rubber stamps {Dawn Hauser for Inkadinkado, JudiKins, Wendi Speciale Designs}

ink {Color Box Chalk}

acrylic paint {Delta, Making Memories}

paintbrush

ultra-thick designer tacky glue

Perfect Paper Adhesive

UHU glue stick

basic tool kit

1 • Apply paper to box

Measure the sides of your box and cut pieces of decorative paper to the correct sizes. Use Perfect Paper Adhesive to adhere the paper to each side of the box.

2 • Add paper strip and buttons

Cut a narrow strip of paper to create a border and adhere it to the sides of the box with Perfect Paper, about ½" (1cm) down from the top of the box. Glue on randomly spaced buttons in colors that complement the motif of the paper you chose. Add paint to the edges of the box and to the box top.

3 • Paint chipboard letters for title

Lay chipboard letters to spell out the title of your book-in-a-box on your work surface. Paint them with a bright acrylic paint color using a small paintbrush. Allow the letters to dry.

4 • Decorate box top

Glue a piece of rickrack along the narrow wooden border of the box top with tacky glue. Decorate the slider top of the box with a picture and some lettering. Glue on the painted chipboard letters with tacky glue, and add a button tied with decorative ribbon or string as a finishing touch.

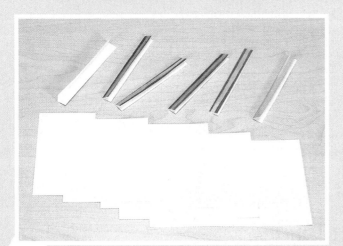

5 • Cut pages and borders for book

To create the accordion book that goes inside the box, you will need to cut cardstock pages and scrapbook paper hinges. Cut ivory cardstock pages as follows: 2¾" x 4½" (7cm x 11cm); 4" x 4½" (10cm x 11cm); 5¼" x 4½" (13cm x 11cm); 6½" x 4½" (16cm x 11cm) and 7½" x 4½" (19cm x 11cm). To make the hinges, cut six strips of the patterned paper used on the cover to 1" x 4½" (3cm x 11cm) and fold each strip in half vertically.

6 • Begin to connect pages

Start with the smallest cardstock panel and connect it to the next smallest page by attaching a hinge strip to one side of each page with a glue stick. The page edges should meet up in the fold of the strip.

7 • Continue connecting pages

Continue connecting pages with hinges, working from the smaller pages toward the larger pages.

8 • Finish connecting pages

When all of the pages are connected, the accordion shape will have a small page in the middle at the top of the book and the largest page will be at the bottom. To finish the accordion book, glue a final folded hinge onto the bare edge of the smallest top panel.

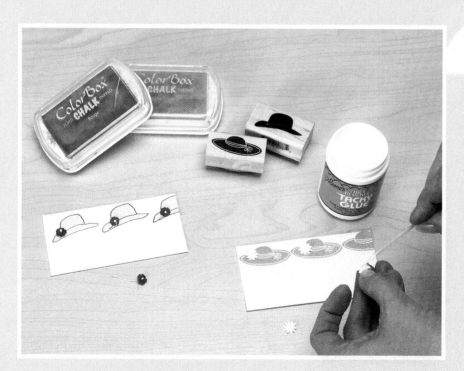

9 • Create stamped pages

Cut small pieces of cardstock to add to the book's pages. Stamp images that support the theme onto the borders. Here, I've used colored ink to stamp hats on the borders of these pages. If you like, you can outline the stamped images with black pen (as I did with the green hats at left). You can also glue on tiny dimensional elements, such as miniature flowers. Fill the book with photos, paper, ribbon and trims, stamps and embellishments to tie in with the box photo and title.

Oh, Bandana!

by Carol

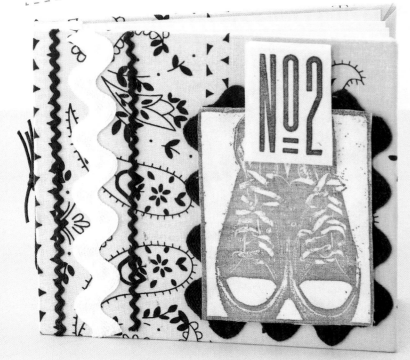

The inspiration for these books came from a recent family trip when my daughter and I came across a huge selection of bandanas in a store called The Mercantile. Both of us were like children in a candy store and added quite a few bandanas to our collections. While driving to our next destination, I thought of using the bandanas to make covers for handmade books to commemorate the trip—funky travel journals. The journals are small and easy to fill, making this a satisfying project to complete quickly.

Art Supplies

GENERAL MATERIALS

book board

bandana

cardstock

waxed linen or embroidery floss

sewing needle

awl

UHU glue stick

basic tool kit

NO. 2 BOOK

wide and narrow rickrack

rubber stamps {Postmodern Design, Stampers Anonymous}

ink {Crafter's}

VACATION BOOK

fabric

flowers {Prima}

mini brads {Coffee Break Design}

vacation charm {Karen Foster Design}

rickrack

MADRID BOOK

bosher {Bazzill}

chipboard letters {Heidi Swapp}

acrylic paint {Making Memories}

flower {Prima}

mini brads {Coffee Break Design}

rickrack

Make it Yours

Because these books are so easy to make and the colors and patterns of bandanas are so varied, they're great gifts. Chronicle an event such as a birthday party, sporting event, special anniversary or new home and use a bright and fun coordinating bandana to cover the book. Layer various bandanas of different colors or weave them together and glue to the top of the cover for lots of color and texture.

1 • Cover book board with bandanas

Cut two pieces of book board to 5⅛" x 6¼" (13cm x 16cm). To cover the book boards with the bandana cloth, lay one piece of board on the cloth and cut around it, leaving about 1½" (4cm) of fabric on all four sides. Glue the cover onto the board with a glue stick or fabric adhesive. Fold the corners onto the back of the board and glue them in place.

2 • Roll sides to finish covering book board

After all four corners are adhered, apply glue to the excess pieces and stand the book cover up on end. Roll the book board so that the fabric stretches tautly and evenly. Brayer the fabric in place. Repeat steps one and two to create the back cover for the book.

4 • Fold binding accordion style

After scoring the paper, you will have five fold lines and six panels. Fold the paper along the lines accordion style and burnish well with your bone folder on the fold lines.

3 • Score lines for accordion binding

To create the accordion to be used as the binding for the pages, cut a piece of cardstock to 5" x 4½" (13cm x 11cm). Using a bone folder and a ruler or the scoring blade on your paper cutter, score a line every ¾" (2cm) along the wider side of the paper.

5 • Begin to create book pages

To create folded panel pages, cut cardstock into 4⅞" x 12" (12cm x 30cm) pieces. Fold each cardstock piece in half and burnish the fold with the bone folder. Each panel should be 4⅞" x 6" (12cm x 15cm). Create three folded page panels for a total of six pages.

6 • Poke holes in pages and accordion binding

To attach the pages into the accordion folds, place the folded edge of each folded panel against the matching fold of the accordion panel (i.e. mountain-to-mountain fold). Create three holes with an awl through the two fold lines simultaneously. One hole should be in the center and the other two holes should be about 1" (3cm) from the top and bottom of the panel.

7 • Begin pamphlet stitch

To stitch the pages in place, use a pamphlet stitch (see Bookmaking Techniques, page 122). Using waxed linen or embroidery floss, bring the needle from the outside of the fold and through the center hole, leaving a 3" (8cm) tail. Carry the waxed linen along inside the fold and then poke the needle up through the top hole.

8 • Make long stitch

Carry the waxed linen along the entire length of the accordion binding on the outside of the book and then thread the needle through the bottom hole (this will be a long stitch) to the inside of the fold.

9 • Finish pamphlet stitch

Bring the needle up through the middle hole to the top of the fold again. Your starting thread and ending thread should be on opposite sides of the long stitch. Tie the ends of the waxed linen in a square knot, making sure to tie the knot around the long stitch. Repeat the pamphlet stitch for the other two folds in the accordion binding.

10 • Apply glue to first page of book

Slide a piece of scrap paper under the first page in the book and coat the page with glue.

11 • Adhere first page to front cover

Smooth the glue-coated front page to the inside of the front cover of the book. Repeat with the back page of the book, adhering it to the back cover.

12 • Decorate front cover of book

Decorate the front cover of the book to commemorate an event or a trip you have taken.

The Love of Color

by Carol

Gardening is one of my favorite ways to relax—the scents and colors are calming and inspirational. I often photograph flowers at a local nursery or public garden. When I was playing with printing my photos on various papers and surfaces, I discovered that the colors were more vivid on transparencies than on photo paper or cardstock. "Ahhh," I thought, "what can I do with transparent photos that hasn't already been done?" After lots of experimenting, I made this transparent hinged book. Building layers of transparent photos, text and embellishments creates an interesting depth that complements the flowers showcased in the book.

Art Supplies

office supply page protectors

clear plastic report covers

dowel rods

transparencies for ink-jet printers

self-adhesive transparencies {Grafix}

white cardstock

ghost letters and flower {Heidi Swapp}

clear tags {American Tag Company}

index tabs {Creative Imaginations}

monogram letter {EK Success}

rub-on letters {L'il Davis}

paper clips or index clips

alcohol inks {Studio 2, Ranger}

felt squares

rubber stamp
{A Stamp in the Hand}

ink {StazOn}

pink acrylic paint
{Making Memories}

acrylic paints in other colors
{Delta}

paintbrushes

Diamond Glaze

rubbing alcohol

misting bottle

basic tool kit

Make it Yours

Transparent art is a wonderful way to experiment with layers. Try starting with a piece of a lightly scripted printed acetate, layer on a transparent photo, then top it off with another piece of acetate printed with a bold title. I look at using transparencies as the old-fashioned way to create pieces similar to the digital art being produced by many memory artists today.

1 • Create hinges

Cut pliable page protectors into 25 1" x 3" (3cm x 8cm) strips. To create hinge pieces, roll the little strips in half and adhere the ends with an adhesive such as Diamond Glaze. Use an index clip or a paper clip to hold each hinge in place until the adhesive dries.

2 • Begin to construct pages

Cut 6" x 6" (15cm x 15cm) pages from clear plastic report covers (each book page requires two plastic pages). Lay two of the plastic pages on your work surface and place three hinges on top of the left-hand page and two hinges on top of the right-hand page with the loops facing toward each other. The loops on each page should be staggered so that the two loops on the right page fall into the empty spaces between hinges on the left page. Adjust the hinges so that the loop end is slightly larger than the dowel rod you will be inserting in the next step. Glue the hinges in place with a dab of Diamond Glaze. Place two more clear plastic pages on top of the first two pages and their hinges. Secure the stacked pages with clips. Continue to make hinged pages until you have made the total desired amount. (The front and back pages will only have hinges on one side.)

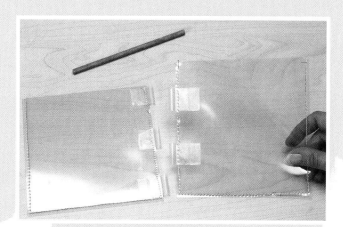

3 • Make pages into pockets

To make the pages into pockets, sew around the left, bottom and right sides of each page, very close to the edge (you may hand-sew or use a sewing machine). Photos and other layers will slip behind the report cover, to be protected from fingerprints and the elements.

4 • Assemble book

Paint as many dowel rods as you'll need with coordinating acrylic paint and allow them to dry. Then simply line up the pages so that the hinges fall in the correct places. Slide a dowel rod down through the hinges on each set of facing pages to form an accordion structure.

5 • Apply alcohol inks to ghost letters

Lay out ghost letters to spell the focal word of your title on a scrap piece of paper. (I chose to spell out "COLOR.") Use alcohol inks on small squares of felt to apply color to each letter.

6 • Create book cover

For the cover, print the first portion of the title directly onto the transparency. I recommend applying inks to the back of the printed transparency to avoid smearing the ink. Swab alcohol inks onto the top portion of your cover with felt. Adhere the letters from step five to the cover with Diamond Glaze.

7 • Make transparency page

You may also use other transparency sheets to slip into your page pockets. To create a mottled effect with alcohol inks, first apply the inks to felt squares and then dab the color onto the transparency. Incorporate one or more additional colors in the same way, blending the colors together if you like.

8 • Spray on alcohol

Fill a small misting bottle with rubbing alcohol and squirt some on the still-wet alcohol ink to create an interesting mottled effect.

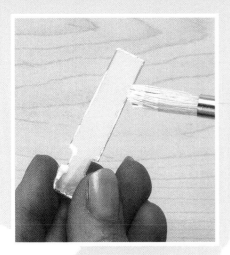

9. Create painted tabs and letters

You may also want to add painted tabs to your pages. Simply cut transparencies down to tab size (or use a premade piece) and paint them with acrylic paint for an opaque look. Paint ghost letters as well, or simply outline them with paint or ink to give them dimension.

10. Create inside pages

Create inside pages for the book to go along with the theme you chose. On the left is a page I made by printing an image with text directly onto a transparency sheet. Behind the transparency sheet is a piece of cardstock drybrushed with pink paint. To create the page on the right, I simply cut a piece of scrapbook paper to 6" x 6" (15cm x 15cm), added some journaling and an image, and slid it into the pocket. I then printed letters directly onto a transparency page and added that sheet on top of the paper in the pocket.

Other Ideas

11. Continue to fill book

To make pages like these, print images and text onto ink-jet transparencies. Add tags, index tabs and ghost letters outlined with paint to finish the pages. Your images will "pop" if you insert 6" x 6" (15cm x 15cm) pieces of white cardstock behind the transparent photos.

More Embellishments

Embellishments such as transparent coin envelopes, clear and printed tabs, and ghost letters and shapes allow for variety in filling your book. They're also great for layering and adding dimension.

Imagine

I am a rusted and aged metal fanatic. My parents and in-laws cannot understand why I spend money on rusty and old-looking things. "Why waste your money on something that looks like it went through the war?" they ask. I don't know what exactly attracts me to weather-worn metal. Maybe it's that the aged look gives the piece a history and a life of its own. Whatever the reason, it's hard for me to resist. When I was browsing through Santa Fe galleries and began taking photos of the amazing metal sculptures, gates and signs, I decided to create an appropriate metal structure to house my wonderful memories.

by Carol

metal horse sculpture

Art Supplies

galvanized metal pieces

book board

fabric

cardstock for pages

grommets {Prym-Dritz}

thin rusted wire

waxed linen thread

rusted metal vines {USArtQuestv}

pewter frame and "IMAGINE" charm {Maude & Millie}

decorative fabric strips

white acrylic paint {Delta}

foam paintbrush

fine-grit sandpaper

bookmaker's punch or large eyelet punch

hammer

tapestry needle

decorative-edge scissors

tacky glue

E6000 glue

basic tool kit

1 • Sand and paint metal covers

Sand the metal pieces that will become the front and back covers of the book with fine-grit sandpaper. Paint the metal pieces with white acrylic paint, using a foam brush. You may paint both sides of each piece, if desired.

2 • Create book board hinges

Cut two pieces of book board the same length as the metal and to a width of 1½" (4cm). The book board pieces will be the hinge pieces that allow the book to be easily opened. Punch three holes into the middle of the book board in a vertical row using a heavy-duty bookmaker's punch.

Make it Yours

Metal books make great masculine books. For example, instead of using a cottage white chenille for the hinge piece like I did in this sample, use burlap, heavy wool flannel or a piece of leather. Tie the book together with pieces of string, hemp or leather. The book cover may be rusted with a rusting kit available at many craft stores, or painted with acrylic paint in a color that coordinates with the fabric.

3 • Adhere fabric to book

Cut two pieces of fabric (a heavy upholstery fabric was used in the sample due to the weight of the metal) to cover the hinges and overlap the metal on the front and back covers about ¾" (2cm). Coat the hinge and the metal that will be covered with fabric with tacky glue, and adhere the fabric. Allow the glue to dry.

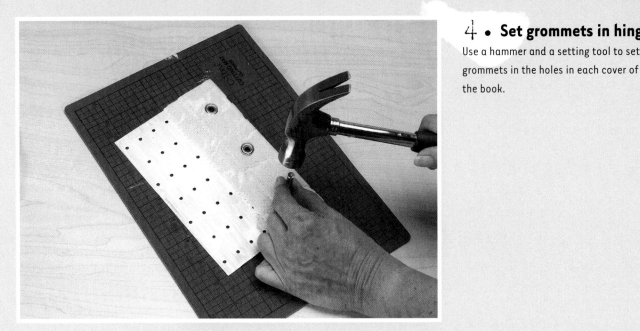

4 • Set grommets in hinges

Use a hammer and a setting tool to set grommets in the holes in each cover of the book.

5 • Make book pages

Cut pages from complementary shades of cardstock, and score them with a bone folder or scoring blade at the hinge point so they will open smoothly. Punch holes in the left margin to align with the grommets in the covers.

6 • Assemble book

Assemble the book by aligning the front and back covers with the pages you created. Tie them all together with torn decorative fabric. In this sample, a basic square knot was used. However, depending upon the look of the project, you can tie bows or use ribbon.

7 • Add stitching to cover

Thread a tapestry needle with sturdy waxed linen. Stitch through the fabric and the existing holes of the metal with the waxed linen. A basic running stitch was used in this sample. This stitching helps secure the fabric to the metal.

8 • Stitch with wire

Decorate the top and bottom of the front cover by "sewing" a blanket stitch trim with thin rusted wire. Blanket stitches are often used by quilters and seamstresses to decoratively finish the edge of a piece.

9 • Add metal embellishments to cover

To finish the book, glue metal embellishments onto the cover using E6000. Allow the glue to dry.

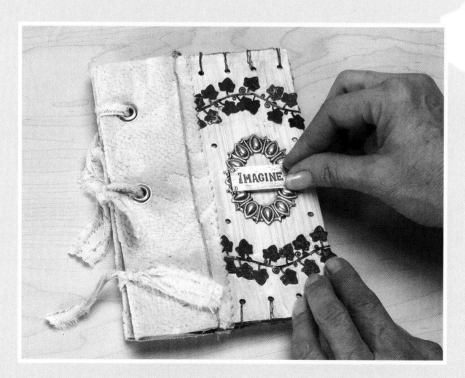

Entrances

by Carol

Great American literary critic and writer Joseph Campbell thought the best way to make society better was to better yourself. "When you follow your bliss," he wrote, "doors will open where you would not have thought there would be doors; and where there wouldn't be a door for anyone else." I've always believed that doors have special significance, and I'd been wanting to visit Santa Fe for years because it's known for its gorgeous and plentiful gates and doors. This spring we took a trip to Santa Fe and Albuquerque, and my thirst for entrances was finally quenched. I compiled photographs of my favorite doors into this book of Entrances.

Make it Yours

Japanese stab binding books are a mainstay in any handmade book library because they are so versatile and easy to decorate. After you have selected your theme, use papers and book cloth for your covers to pull the look together. The book may be stitched together with ribbon, hemp, twine or flexible wire.

Art Supplies

book board
cardstock
patterned papers {Midori}
wooden gate
metal plaque
{Karen Foster Metals}
key charms {7 Gypsies}
black twine or hemp
gaffer's tape or book tape

binder clips
acrylic paint {Delta}
paintbrush or glue mop
hand drill, Japanese screw punch, or bookmaker's punch and hammer
tapestry needle
PVA glue
E6000 adhesive
basic tool kit

1 • Lay out book board and hinge

Cut book board to the size desired for the covers of your book. In this sample, the book board is 7" x 10" (18cm x 25cm). To create a hinge piece, cut the spine side of the book boards to the size desired. In this sample, the hinge piece is 1¾" x 10" (4cm x 25cm).

To cover the front and back covers, lay the book boards on a sheet of decorative paper, allowing about ¼" (6mm) between the hinge piece and the large cover piece. Cut the paper so that it over-laps the top, bottom and open side of the cover about 1" to 1¼" (3cm to 4cm). The spine side should have enough paper to cover the under side of the hinge. The extra coverage will provide added strength when opening the book.

2 • Miter corners

Apply PVA glue to the book board pieces and adhere them to the paper. Brayer the boards to adhere them well and to remove any air bubbles. Use scissors to cut away all of the corners so that the mitered corners will fold over smoothly.

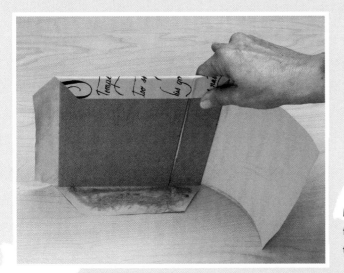

4 • Secure corners

Make sure that the corner pieces are pressed in with either a fingernail or a bone folder. Repeat steps one through four for the back cover of the book.

3 • Roll edges

Roll the book cover up on its end to stretch the paper taut. Work on opposing sides—top first, then bottom, then side to side. Glue the paper in place and brayer it well.

5 • Adhere book tape

Cut a piece of wide book tape or gaffer's tape to a length that is a few inches longer than the height of the book. Adhere the tape to each cover of the book, wrapping the ends around to the back to secure them.

6 • Adhere end papers

Cut coordinating papers to cover the back side of the front and back covers. These papers should be cut to create about a ¼" (6mm) margin on all four sides. Glue the paper in place and brayer well.

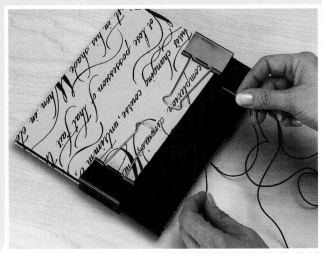

7 • Score pages

Cut cardstock or text-weight (if using for a writing journal) pages for the book. Use a bone folder and a ruler to score a line in the cardstock that corresponds with the cover hinges.

8 • Assemble book

Stack up the book as follows: front cover, inside pages, back cover. Clip the covers and the pages together with binder clips. Measure and mark stitch holes along the hinge piece. I used five holes. Mark one hole in the center, one 1" (3cm) from the top, one 1" (3cm) from the bottom and the other two centered in between the existing marks.

With a hand drill, Japanese screw punch (a high-quality punch), or a bookmaker's punch and hammer, create stitching holes at each mark. (It will take some effort to make the holes if your book is thick.)

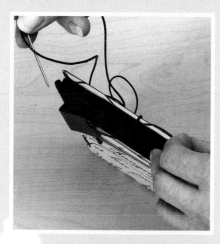

9 • Begin to stitch book

Keep the binder clips in place until stitching is done. Cut twine or hemp to about seven lengths of the book. Thread a tapestry needle with a large eye, using a single thread and no end knot. Start in the middle hole at the back and bring the needle through to the front, leaving about a 3" (8cm) tail.

10 • Continue stitching

Wrap the thread around the spine, into the back center hole again and up to the front. Take the thread to the next hole toward the top. Repeat the process.

11 • Stitch around top of book

Repeat the stitching again at the top hole, and then wrap the thread around the top of the book and back into the top hole again.

12 • Tie off thread

Complete the blanket stitches on the top half of the book and then repeat the process on the bottom half of the book. When stitching is complete, the thread should be at the back of the book. Tie a square knot in the back center hole and trim the thread. Apply a dab of glue to secure the knot.

13 • Decorate front cover of book

Decorate the front cover of the book with a painted gate adhered with E6000. You might add other embellishments, like a metal plaque or some key charms.

Book Arts Gallery

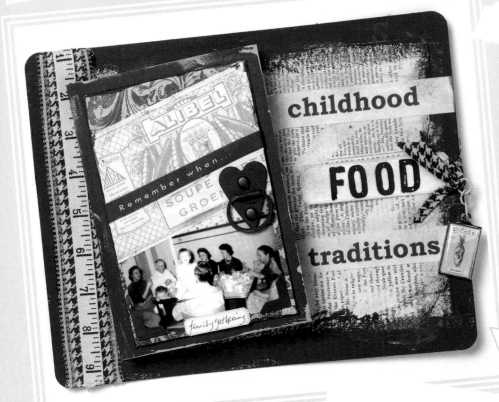

Childhood Food Traditions

Growing up in a Slavic family meant growing up around food and food traditions. The little collection of traditions I chose to fill this book is just the tip of the iceberg of memories I have of family gatherings and rituals involving food. In order to capture as many memories as I could for this layout, I attached an embellished eight-panel accordion to an 11" x 8½" (28cm x 22cm) piece of chipboard that I painted black. I then adhered pages from an old book and used masking tape to peel off portions of the pages. I accented the pages with black and green paints to carry out the color theme.

by Carol Wingert

by Carol Wingert

It's a Girl Thing

The inspiration for this project came from the diversity I saw in my daughter Ashley's shoe collection. As I wrote on one of the pages in the book, "Diversity is not a new term around our house...from combat boots to paddock boots and from flip-flops to dressy mules, Ashley has managed to achieve diversity in her collection of shoes." The amazing variety in shoes definitely speaks to Ashley's varied interests in life. This book is comprised of digital photos that have been manipulated through photo editing software. To alter the appearance of some of the photos, I have changed the color, saturation and hue. I also added computer-generated journaling.

Art File

When I was young, one of my favorite art techniques was to take bright crayons and color all over the surface of my construction paper, then color on top of that with a black crayon, then scratch a picture into the black that revealed my bright colors beneath. Using the clayboard with re-inkers totally captures the scratch art of my elementary school days with a more sophisticated feel.

by Tena Sprenger

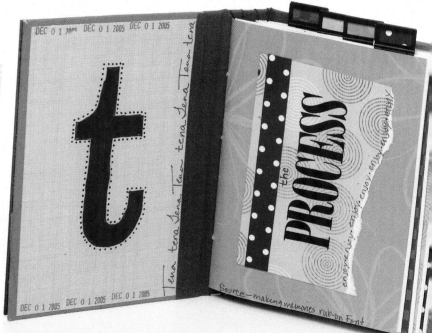

To make your own scratch art, simply stamp images for the covers of your book onto paper and cut them out to use as a template for scratching into the surface of the clayboard. Dust away residue after scratching the surface design and use a toothpick to apply the ink into the scratches. Apply spray fixative to book covers to protect and seal. Use a soft cloth dampened with water to clean up any excess ink. Cover the book board with patterned paper using a glue stick and brayer, and cover the spine area with gaffer's tape. Create signatures using cardstock and patterned paper. Create a sewing template and pierce the book board and signatures, and simply sew in pages to finish.

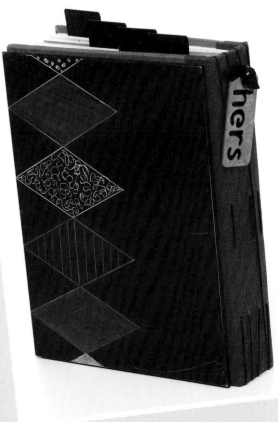

Wall Arts

Some people inspect bookshelves or CD collections to get a feel for what someone is like. For Tena and me, it's the portraits on the walls and the creative displays of personal mementos and family treasures that let us peek into family stories and histories.

As memory artists who have more photos than we can ever hope to fit into a traditional scrapbook, it thrills us to no end to come up with new ways to incorporate our stories, photos and memorabilia into artful and tasteful decorations in our homes. When cruising the aisles of our favorite home décor stores, or flipping through the latest home fashion catalogs, we are constantly having little "light bulb" moments that cause us to imagine the creative possibilities of adding photos or journaling to traditional as well as nontraditional home accents.

Whether it is a window from your local home improvement store altered to create a decorative wall hanging for your child's room or a sophisticated Polaroid image transfer turned framed wall art, we hope this chapter will start your creative wheels turning and will inspire you to surround yourself with the photos and memories you cherish.

Ilse and the Lion Cub

I received quite a windfall when I got a request from the Hannau family to create memory art using the wonderful pictures taken by the photographer and traveler Dr. Hans Hannau throughout his life. When I first saw this photo, taken by Hans of his wife Ilse, I was struck by her youthful beauty and the sense of adventure and exoticism in the scene. I think the words and the background embellishments I chose really capture the moment that Hans found through his lens.

by Carol

Art Supplies

papier mâché wall panel

patterned papers {Foofala}

solid-color cardstock

ribbon and trim {May Art}

rusted iron keys {Maude & Millie}

hat pin {EK Success}

eyelets

brown acrylic paint {Delta}

small paintbrush

eyelet setter

hammer

UHU glue stick

tacky glue

basic tool kit

Make it Yours

As I was making this mini wall hanging, I thought about how fun it would be to create vintage hangings of each of my grandparents to add to my family portrait wall. Can you just see fancy vintage fringe hanging from the bottom and some wonderful twill or ribbon knotted into the top holes to hang the piece? Or, what about a fun arrangement of these papier mâché panels with your children, your parents, or your pets? Can you tell I love these little pieces?

1 • Paint sides of papier mâché panel

Use a small paintbrush to apply brown paint to the edges of a papier mâché panel with a hanger.

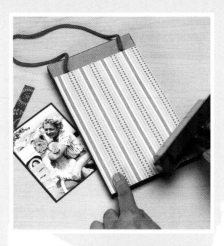

2 • Adhere decorative papers and photo

Use a glue stick to adhere decorative paper to the wall panel. Brayer the paper well. Layer the photo you chose onto a piece of solid-color cardstock, leaving a thin border of paper around the photo. Glue the layered photo to the layout as well. Adhere a thin strip of complementary decorative paper above the hanging holes, as well as a narrow ribbon. Cut the ribbon to go around the grommets.

3 • Add eyelets to ribbon

Use an eyelet setter and a hammer to set eyelets at regular intervals in the ribbon. Or you may buy ribbon with eyelets already set into it.

4 • Tie keys onto ribbon

Thread a key onto a short length of ribbon and tie the ribbon through the first eyelet. Repeat for each eyelet.

5 • Apply ribbon embellishments

Adhere the ribbons and trims around the photo, and glue down the ribbon tied with keys using tacky glue. Hold the ribbon in place for a few seconds until the glue begins to set. Allow the glue to dry completely before hanging.

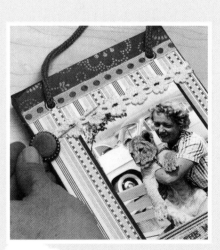

6 • Add hat pin

As a finishing touch, weave a decorative hat pin through one of the trims or ribbons.

Life

by Tena

I am an alphabet junkie! I collect alphabet stamps, and I love incorporating different typographies into artwork. I was shopping in one of my favorite stores when I happened upon these cool letters, and I could instantly picture them as a perfect way to display photos autobiographically. I think it would also be fun to set these letters on a shelf or mantel. Or, you might display letters to spell out a child's name in her room. Simply decorate the letters with words and photos that describe the child.

Art Supplies

galanized steel alphabet letters
(The letter size is 8" [20cm] high and the widths vary based on the letter. The widest is "E" at 4" [11cm] wide. Letters are 1" [3cm] deep.)

alphabet, word and image rub-ons
{Making Memories, 7 Gypsies, Autumn Leaves, Heidi Swapp}

black cardstock

double spiral clips {Making Memories}

acrylic paints {Making Memories}

paintbrush

ink {StazOn Jet Black}

sandpaper

sponge

sealer
{Krylon acrylic matte spray sealer}

E6000 adhesive

Make it Yours

If you love the idea of spelling a name, word or phrase with alphabet letters, consider mounting your letters on a canvas or plaque or setting them on a decorative shelf to give your alphabet art a different look.

1 • Paint edges of letters

Use a paintbrush with black paint to darken the edges of the metal alphabet letters. Use a sponge to lightly sponge on green paint to further distress the letters. Allow the paint to dry.

2 • Apply rub-ons to letters

Apply rub-on letters, words and decorations to embellish the metal letters. Follow the directions on the package as you apply the rub-ons.

3 • Create picture holders

To make photo clips, sand down the shiny surface of a double spiral paper clip and then ink the surface with black ink to match the metal letters. Bend the double spiral clips into an L shape and glue them to the metal letters with a strong epoxy glue, such as E6000, where photos will be clipped on.

4 • Spray letters with sealer

When all of the rub-ons and photo clips have been applied, seal the surface of the metal letters with Krylon matte spray sealer to keep the paint from peeling and the rub-ons from flaking.

5 • Add backing to photos

Choose the photos you'd like to use and make copies of them. Lay them all on a sturdy sheet of black cardstock and trace around each one. Cut out the backing paper and glue it to the corresponding photo. Slip the photos into the wire holders. You can switch the photos to keep your display current.

The Arboretum

by Carol

These photos were taken at The Arboretum outside of Phoenix, Arizona (yes, you can grow plants other than cacti in Arizona). I love the colors, the rusted iron and old stone in these images. My initial thought was to incorporate my photos into a large frame, but after a trip to my local home improvement store, I decided to use a cabinet door instead. After some sanding, painting and distressing, I had the perfect background for my canvases and photos. Simple to make and dramatic to display—my favorite.

Make it Yours

Shabby chic and flea market fanatics can use an antique or well-worn cabinet to save time. Make sure the surface of the cabinet door is clean and that the areas where glue will be applied are free of peeling paint. If you favor a clean, more contemporary look, buy a new cabinet door and keep your canvases simple and uncluttered. Add contemporary hardware, if desired.

Art Supplies

cabinet door

four 5" x 7" {13cm x 18cm} flat canvases {Fredrix}

used book pages

old labels

door handle

rubber stamps {Stampers Anonymous, Postmodern Design}

ink {Ancient Page}

black acrylic paint {Making Memories}

paintbrush

picture-hanging hardware

PVA glue

basic tool kit

1 • Paint canvases

Paint four canvases to coordinate with the photos you have chosen—a darker color generally works best. Allow the paint to dry.

2 • Adhere papers to canvases

Cover a large portion of each canvas with pages from old books, dictionaries, encyclopedias or any other decorative papers with wording. Glue the pages into place with PVA glue, and brayer over them so they adhere well.

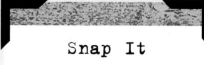

Snap It

Frame and crop your subject matter with the camera. Although you can crop with a photo editing program, the best quality photos will come from cropping at the time your photo is shot. And by focusing on good composition within the lens, you are training yourself to take better photos.

❧ *Zoom in on your subject matter, especially if you're photographing people.*

❧ *Take lots of pictures. Even professional photographers say they take lots of shots to get the really good ones.*

3 • Adhere pictures to canvases and add stamping

Print photos that have been sized to fit the canvas onto matte, heavy-weight photo paper. Glue each photo over the book pages already adhered to the canvases. Add rubber stamping directly onto the photos, as well as labels and other elements that coordinate with the photos.

4 • Adhere canvases to cabinet

To finish the cabinet door, simply adhere each canvas to the wooden surface. Canvases may be glued directly onto the cabinet with a heavy-duty glue available at hardware stores, or they may be glued to another surface, such as a block of wood or framed canvas, so that it protrudes from the cabinet. Add a handle to the front of the cabinet and picture-hanging hardware to the back to complete the project.

Samantha

by Tena

Sami is such a little cutie, her smile lights up any room and her giggles make me laugh. She loves to clap her hands and dance, and blow kisses. She has wonderful soft baby skin and silky hair. I love her lots. ♡

Samantha '03

My favorite portraits are usually not the posed shots taken at the studio, but rather the ones that capture natural smiles and expressions. I have had the joy of regularly photographing my niece Samantha over the past year—her little smile is so infectious and her eyes always have the sparkle that comes from discovering new things every day. Using a pen on top of the photograph gave me the ability to hang this on the wall like a portrait, but also to add my thoughts as I would on a scrap-book page, so I never forget her personality as a toddler.

Make it Yours

I loved the crisp look of my photo when I printed it on a transparency and then mounted it on white paper. For a more edgy or vintage look, try using gel medium and a transparency photo to image transfer your photo directly onto the canvas.

Art Supplies

art canvas {Fredrix}

transparency {Apollo}

patterned paper {Creative Imaginations}

white and black cardstock

fabric ribbon

white glaze pen {Sakura}

acrylic paint {Making Memories}

foam brush or paintbrush

adhesive tape {Tombow}

UHU glue stick

basic tool kit

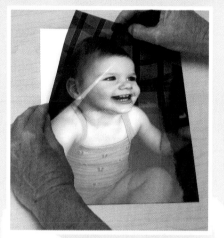

1 • Paint canvas

Paint only the edges and the sides of a 8½" x 11" (22cm x 28cm) canvas with a shade of acrylic paint that coordinates with the paper you choose for your background.

2 • Mount photo on cardstock

Print a high contrast photo with a relatively dark background onto a transparency sheet. Mount the transparency on top of white cardstock with adhesive tape to create the illusion of a super-crisp black-and-white photo. Trim the white cardstock so that it is the exact same size as the transparency sheet.

3 • Add journaling

Use a white gel glaze pen to journal directly onto the surface of the photo transparency. The writing from the glaze pen will have a slightly raised surface on the photo transparency sheet.

4 • Mount transparency photo on cardstock

With tape adhesive, mount the transparency onto a piece of black cardstock that is just slightly larger than the transparency sheet to create a black border.

5 • Finish wall art

Trim a piece of patterned paper to fit the canvas, leaving a small edge of painted canvas showing. Adhere the paper to the painted canvas with a glue stick. Layer the cardstock-backed transparency on top of the patterned paper, adhering it with a glue stick and brayering over it to secure it. To finish the artwork, tie a piece of coordinating ribbon or fabric in a bow around the lower portion of the piece.

Cousins

by Tena

Wandering around in a home improvement store can be a creative adventure, especially with the current trend of bringing the outdoors inside. On one of my visits, I found a blank white ceramic address frame. Of course, I had no intention of using it to actually display my house number—half the fun of memory art is creatively repurposing standard objects. I instantly saw it as a picture frame with the photo transferred directly onto it. The final result is a vibrantly colorful tribute to my niece and nephew and their love of the outdoors.

Art Supplies

ceramic address frame {Capital Products}

ceramic tile

metal word for title {Senti-metals}

ink-jet image transfer paper {Lazertran}

acrylic paint {Folk Art}

paintbrush

sandpaper

matte finish paint sealer {Krylon}

dish of water

E6000 glue

basic tool kit

Make it Yours

Tile and other types of ceramics are great for image transfers. Consider using this same technique to create coasters or plates. Transferring photos to coasters is a great way to tell a story—use wedding photos or leftover pictures from your childhood. Then any guest who shares a cool drink will get a glimpse into your life.

1 • Assemble supplies

This is what the address frame looks like before it is altered. Have a piece of ceramic tile cut to the correct size at a home improvement store. The tile used here is a standard 12" x 12" (30cm x 30cm) ceramic floor tile cut down to fit the frame.

2 • Sand and paint frame

Sand the address frame to remove the glossy finish and to prepare the frame to be painted. Lightly pounce paint onto the surface of the frame. Allow the paint to dry. When the paint is fully dry, sand the frame to create a distressed look.

3 • Paint with second color and sand

Apply a light coat of a complementary color of paint to the frame surface. Allow the paint to dry and sand the surface again lightly. Seal the paint on the frame with a spray matte finish and set it aside to dry.

Image Transfer

Lazertran is a great product to use when transferring images to many nonporous surfaces. Consider transferring images to metal, glass or ceramic surfaces with Lazertran. Lazertran is available for ink-jet as well as for laser printers.

4 • Prepare photo for transfer

Print the photo you'd like to use in the frame onto Lazertran ink-jet paper, following the manufacturer's instructions. Measure your frame opening to be sure that you print your photo to fit the tile and opening. Let the image dry for 30 minutes to set it. Trim the photo to a size that fits the ceramic tile.

5 • Submerge image in water

Submerge the image in room temperature water for one minute, or until the decal floats away from the paper.

6 • Transfer image to tile

Very carefully lift the paper from the water and slide the image onto the surface of the tile. Try to avoid touching the image decal any more than necessary to avoid rips and tears caused by overhandling.

7 • Smooth out image

Moisten your fingers or use a wet sponge to carefully smooth any wrinkles or bumps from the transferred image. Let the image dry overnight. Spray the image with matte finish spray or clear polyurethane to seal the image onto the ceramic tile.

8 • Adhere tile to frame and add metal title

Glue the tile into the frame using E6000 epoxy glue. Lightly sand the metal word and paint it with white paint. Let the paint dry and sand the word. Distress the edges of the title by painting it with a contrasting color of paint. Lightly sand the edges once the paint has dried. Seal the paint on the title word with spray matte finish and let it dry. Adhere the title to the tile and frame with E6000 epoxy glue.

She's All Girl

by Carol

One day, while searching through my paint drawer for a certain color, I happened to glance at a porcelain palette dish I use to mix paints. My brain went into the total think mode—how could I use this dish to display a photo or journaling? I came up with the idea of using Lazertran image transfers and little bits of journaling for this very girlie piece of art. Any dish with sections (egg dishes or serving platters for hors d'oeuvres), or even plain white porcelain plates, may be used. Hanging the plates from a holder or placing them on a rack is a great way to display them.

Art Supplies

ceramic palette dish
Alphadotz circles {Scrapworks}
ink-jet image transfer paper {Lazertran}
ribbon {May Arts}
small metal easel *(for display)*
pop dots
acrylic paint {Delta}
ink {Ranger Industries}
paintbrush
makeup sponge
circle punch
basic tool kit

Make it Yours

If you're into another craft, don't hesitate to cross crafting boundaries and incorporate it into a project like this one. For example, if you've dabbled in beading, you're sure to have a million different beads just lying around. Apply a strong glue to each of the round sections and cover them with beads. The central photo will look like the center of a beautiful, glittering flower.

1 • Apply paint to edges of palette dish

Apply brown paint to the edges of a ceramic palette dish in a shabby fashion. Set the dish aside to dry.

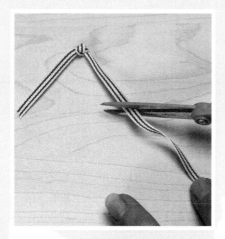

2 • Create ribbon petals

Cut a 3" (8cm) section of ribbon for each outside circle on the palette dish. Create ribbon petals by tying a knot in the center of each ribbon piece. Cross the ends of the ribbon and glue each one to the back of an Alphadotz to create a petal.

3 • Ink edges of Alphadotz

Apply a little brown ink to a makeup sponge and ink the edges of the Alphadotz.

4 • Add pop dots

Remove the backing from the pop dots an adhere a pop dot over the ends of each ribbon on the back of the Alphadotz.

5 • Cut out photo

Scan and resize a photo for the center section of the dish. Print the image onto ink-jet image transfer paper according to the manufacturer's instructions. Allow the image to dry for 30 minutes. Punch out the photo with a circle punch.

6 • Add photo and Alphadotz

Place the image in water for one minute and apply the decal to the center of the palette dish. Dab it with a paper towel to remove moisture and allow it to dry. Peel the backing away from the pop dots and adhere the Alphadotz-and-ribbon petals to the palette dish as shown.

Shy Beauty

by Tena

I love these dramatic photos of my daughter Alyssa taken before a dance recital. They have an artsy quality that made me want to display them rather than put them in my scrapbook. Not long after taking the pictures, I took a Polaroid image transfer class at my local paper arts store, and I was totally hooked on the process and the results. I immediately ordered my own Daylab and started experimenting. The image transfers I was able to produce truly capture the dramatic nature of the pictures while giving them the soft, hazy look produced by the Polaroid film chemicals on watercolor paper.

Make it Yours

I completely love the way the Polaroid image transfer technique softens and adds an artistic effect to my photos. You can create additional effects using Polaroid images like emulsion lifts and Polaroid manipulations. For information on these and other Polaroid techniques, visit the Daylab website at www.daylab.com for step-by-step instructions.

Art Supplies

corrugated cardboard

chipboard

patterned paper {Geneva}

hot-press watercolor paper {Strathmore}

netted sewing thread {Timeless Touches}

Polaroid Daylab

Polaroid 669 film

warm water bath

paper towels

micro-tip pen {Sakura}

paint glaze {Delta}

turquoise acrylic paint {Delta}

paintbrush

adhesive tape

awl

tapestry needle

basic tool kit

1 . Soak paper to prepare for transfer

To prepare watercolor paper to accept the Polaroid image, soak the paper for two minutes in a 160°F (71°C) bath of hot water.

2 . Brayer excess water from paper

Remove the paper from the hot water bath and sandwich it between two paper towels. Brayer over the top paper towel to remove excess water from the paper. Set the watercolor paper aside on a clean surface.

High Contrast

When selecting photos to use for image transfer with the Daylab, consider using images that are high-contrast with a lighter background. When the photo subject and the back-ground are the same general color, the image transfer may look muddy and unclear.

3 . Make film of image

Load the Polaroid Daylab with 669 film. Place your 4" x 6" (10cm x 15cm) photo face down on the glass of the Polaroid Daylab, making sure that the image is squarely within the frame. Place the black cover over the photo. Press the exposure button on the machine to expose the film. If you are unhappy with the exposure you made, simply adjust the exposure dial to improve the picture quality.

4 • Transfer image to watercolor paper

Pull the film out from the Daylab and allow the film to process for only 15 seconds. At the end of 15 seconds, remove the paper covering from the film and place it image side down onto the prepared watercolor paper. Brayer the image onto the paper using medium pressure for about two minutes to ensure a good transfer. Gently remove the negative and allow the image transfer to air dry. Repeat steps one through four for three more images.

5 • Add paint accents to edges of transfers

To pick up some of the color made by the chemicals during the transfer process, drybrush a little turquoise paint around the edges of each picture. Mix two parts of paint with one part of glaze to create a sheer wash of paint.

6 • Mount image transfers onto chipboard

Mount the image transfers onto a piece of chipboard with adhesive tape.

Try and Try Again

Creating image transfers with the Daylab and 669 film is by no means an exact science. For example, waiting 15 seconds to remove the covering from the film is a general rule, but you may find that 17 or 12 seconds works better with some photos to produce an image you like. One result of brayering the image onto the watercolor paper is that some of the sepia and turquoise colors will squish outside of the edge of the photos...I really like this effect! If you'd like to minimize this effect, use slightly lighter pressure when brayering.

8 • Add decorative stitches

Thread a piece of netted thread or fiber onto a large needle and stitch through the holes you made with the awl, creating Xs.

7 • Poke holes with awl

Use an awl to poke sets of two holes on the borders between the image transfers where you would like to add stitching.

9 • Add text

Use an archival ink pen to add hand journaling to the image transfers. Mount the image transfers onto a piece of complementary patterned paper backed with cardboard. Brayer over the piece to secure all layers together.

My Girl for All Seasons

by Miley Johnson

I created this piece for my four-year-old daughter's room. Ladybugs, butterflies and all things pink, blue and yellow decorate her room, and I wanted to make something that would work well with those motifs. I kept this very whimsical and shabby to fit the mood of a toddler/little girl's room, and I added photos to give it a polished look.

To make your own display window, paint a window frame and stamp a phrase along the bottom with permanent ink. Then paint wooden accents and set them aside. Cover precut photo mats with patterned paper and add word accents. Glue the photo mats and wooden accents to the front of the window, on top of the glass. To display the photos, layer them with twill on foam core and mount them behind the glass, lining up the photos with the photo mats. Finish by adding button accents and securing the foam core backing with a staple gun.

by Carol Wingert

WHAT HAPPENED?

After years of dressing Ashley in pretty pink dresses, overalls, you name it, she starts dressing herself in blue denim. What happened? Did I overload the pink thing and turn her off for life? Is this my fault? I dont know what happened to my girlie girl but, somewhere along the way, Ashley developed a style that was comfortable for her. And, in reality, isn't that what's really important anyway? Ashley, enjoy your style!

Ashley Then and Now

When you start to chronicle the life of your children, sometimes you are hit with the obvious. At some point, something happened along the way to change the appearance of one of those children. This observation was what inspired me to create a collaged canvas of Ashley, from her childhood girlie style to her current, more tomboyish look. I created a template of a dress, cut it out of vintage-looking paper, added the story in my handwriting, and "hung" the dress on a small quilter's hanger. I used pink themed paper on the girlie side and blue themed paper on the tomboy side in keeping with her clothing colors. Can I let you in on the secret behind the change? It's Mimi, the beautiful gray pony in the photo with Ashley. Horses and pink dresses just don't mix.

by Tena Sprenger

No Day Like Today

I love quotes, and I love finding uses for my scrapbooking supplies when creating home décor! I was shopping in my favorite home décor store when I saw a framed quote in a bead trim frame. I got to thinking, why not pick my own favorite quote or saying and then use alphabet letters and my own supplies to spell out the quote?

Pick your own favorie quotation and make your own framed art. Take a frame apart and use cardboard backing to mount your design, making sure to measure for detail placement and paper cutting. Cut background patterned paper to size for your cardboard backing, and adhere it with a glue stick and brayer. Select paint colors and use a small brush to apply acrylic paint to the bead trim on the inner edge of the picture frame. Allow it to dry. Create the die cut flower using Quickutz die cutting hand tool and die. Select alphabet letters to spell out your words, and apply ink and paint where desired. Adhere all framed elements with strong glue to ensure long-lasting adhesion when hanging on the wall.

About Our Guest Artists

Kelly Anderson has been published in various publications, including *Creating Keepsakes*, *Paper Arts*, *Simple Scrapbooks*, and *Better Homes and Gardens*. Her work is featured in *Full Circle*, *Hot Looks for Scrapbooks*, *7 Gypsies in Paris*, *CK Elements* and *CK Artistic Effects*. She is also in the CK Hall of Fame 2002. Kelly and her husband Tony live in Tempe, Arizona, and are expecting their first child in just weeks!

Jessie Baldwin has wanted to be an artist since childhood. She considers each 12" x 12" (30cm x 30cm) page her canvas and proudly displays much of her art on the walls of her house, instead of in albums. She has been recognized for her work in several major industry contests: as a finalist in the 2004 Make it Meaningful Contest, one of ten winners in the international 2005 Memory Makers Masters Competition, and an Honorable Mention in the 2005 Creating Keepsakes Hall of Fame. Jessie has been published in *Creating Keepsakes*; *Scrapbooks, Etc.*; *Memory Makers*; *Legacy Art Magazine*; *PaperKuts*; *Scrapbook Trends*; and more. She lives in Las Vegas with her husband Rick and her two children, Violet and Riley.

Katherine Brooks has been scrapbooking and creating altered art for over eight years. As a full-time employee of Deluxe Designs, Katherine has authored over four idea books, and she also travels to teach scrapbooking techniques all over the US. In 2004, Katherine became a Creating Keepsakes Hall of Famer and is published in numerous scrapbooking magazines. When she's not traveling, Katherine enjoys spending time with her husband John of eleven years, and her two children, Meghan (9) and Matt (5).

Miley Johnson jumped into scrapbooking eight years ago, and through that medium has discovered her true passion to create. With four children, a husband, a dog and a cat, there is no limit to the subjects and topics she records. Miley is a 2004 Creating Keepsakes Hall of Fame winner, as well as the grand prize winner of Chatterbox's Make it Meaningful $10,000 contest. She is also a Garden Girl for the popular scrapbooking website www.2peasinabucket.com.

Pam Kopka is a freelance artist and contributor to *Creating Keepsakes Artistic Effects*, *The Pocket Book* and *Totally Titles II*. She was a Creating Keepsakes Hall of Fame winner 2004, and received the Creating Keepsakes honorable mention in 2003 and 2002. Pam, a kindergarten teacher, loves to spend time camping with her family. Her hobbies include: sewing, painting, mixed media art, photography, fishing, and, of course, scrapbooking.

Heidi Swapp lives in Mesa, Arizona, with her husband of eleven years and their three children: Colton (8), Cory (6) and Quincy (4). Heidi loves scrapbooking—maybe a little too much! She has been obsessed with it for at least seven years, and she liked it a lot for a long time before that! She has traveled the globe teaching and sharing her ideas for the last few years and has been busily creating her own signature line of scrapbooking supplies...if for no other reason than to indulge her own inner scrapper. To see more of her work, visit her website, www.heidiswapp.com.

Bookmaking Techniques

All of the handmade books featured in the Book Arts section are simply constructed and quite easy to make, even for beginners. Some of the books require some simple techniques for binding or for decoration. The bookmaking basics are outlined here.

Covering the Book Board

For almost any book you make, one of the first things you'll do is cover book board to make the covers. Just follow a couple of simple steps to cover book board correctly: secure the corners and roll the sides.

1. Lay out paper and book board

Cut book board to the size desired for the covers of your book. To create a hinge piece, cut the spine side of the book board to the size desired. To cover the front and back covers, lay the book boards on a sheet of paper, allowing about ¼" (6mm) between the hinge piece and the large cover piece. Cut the paper so that it overlaps the top, bottom and open side of the cover about 1" to 1¼" (3cm to 4cm). The spine side should have enough paper to cover the underside of the hinge. The extra coverage will provide added strength when opening the book.

2. Miter corners

Use scissors to cut away all of the corners so that the mitered corners will fold over the book board smoothly.

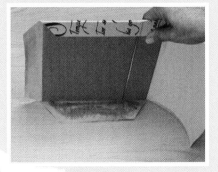

3. Roll edges

Apply a glue stick or PVA glue to the paper. Roll the book cover up on its end to stretch the paper taut. Work on opposing sides— top first, then bottom, then side to side. Glue the paper in place and brayer it well to adhere the paper securely and to remove any air bubbles.

4. Secure corners

Make sure that the corner pieces are pressed in with either a fingernail or a bone folder. Repeat steps one through four for the back cover of the book.

Pamphlet Stitch

Use this simple and functional stitch to bind a signature to a spine. With just a few quick stitches and a knot, you'll create a secure and attractive binding.

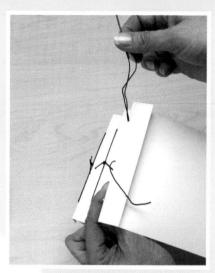

1 • Begin pamphlet stitch

Create an accordion-fold book and then create a smaller version to use for binding the pages. Fit the two pieces together so that the accordion pages fit into the accordion binding. Use an awl to poke three evenly spaced holes in each fold. Using waxed linen or embroidery floss, bring the needle from the outside of the fold and through the center hole, leaving a 3" (8cm) tail. Carry the waxed linen along inside the fold and then poke the needle up through the top hole.

2 • Make long stitch

Carry the waxed linen along the entire length of the accordion binding on the outside of the book and then thread the needle through the bottom hole (this will be a long stitch) to the inside of the fold.

3 • Finish pamphlet stitch

Bring the needle up through the middle hole to the top of the fold again. Your starting thread and ending thread should be on opposite sides of the long stitch. Knot the ends of the threads together to finish the stitch. Repeat the stitch for all of the folds.

Blanket Stitch

Blanket stitches are often used by quilters and seamstresses to decoratively finish the edge of a piece. Its effect on book edges is equally lovely.

1 • Stitch around book edge

Thread a needle with a large eye with a length of rusted wire (or any other heavy stringing material). Bring the needle through the first hole from the back to the front of the book, leaving a short tail. Tie the end of the wire to the working wire to secure it. Bring the needle around the top of the book to the back and pull the needle through the second hole from back to front. Bring the needle through the loop that forms at the top of the book and tighten it to create the first blanket stitch.

2 • Continue blanket stitch

Working to the right, continue to blanket stitch along the top edge of the book. Repeat for any other edges of the projects, as you like.

Resources

All of the materials used in the projects in this book can be purchased at your local craft, fabric, hardware, home improvement, scrapbooking, rubber-stamping or discount department stores. If you are unable to find what you need at a local store, contact the manufacturers listed below for a retailer near you.

Papers and Embellishments

7 gypsies
www.7gypsies.com
paper, embellishments

American Tag Company
www.americantag.net
tags, embellishments

Anna Griffin, Inc.
www.annagriffin.com
paper, embellishments

Autumn Leaves
(Foof-a-la and MOD)
www.autumnleaves.com
paper and embellishments

Basic Grey
www.basicgrey.com
paper, embellishments

Bazzill Basics
www.bazzillbasics.com
cardstock, embellishments

Cavallini and Co.
www.cavallini.com
stationery, paper, gifts

Chatterbox, Inc.
www.chatterboxinc.com
paper, embellishments

Creative Imaginations, Inc.
www.cigift.com
embellishments

Deluxe Designs
www.deluxecuts.com
die cuts, embellishments

Design Originals
www.d-originals.com
paper, embellishments

DMD Industries, Inc.
www.dmdind.com
paper

EK Success
www.eksuccess.com
paper, embellishments

Ellison
www.ellison.com
die cuts

Heidi Swapp
www.heidiswapp.com
embellishments, chipboard products, foam stamps, masks

Iota
www.everyiota.com
paper

Junkitz
www.junkitz.com
embellishments

K&Company
www.kandcompany.com
paper, embellishments

KI Memories
www.kimemories.com
scrapbook paper

Kangaroo and Joey
www.kangarooandjoey.com
paper and embellishments

Karen Foster Design
www.karenfosterdesign.com
embellishments

Lara's Crafts
www.larascrafts.com
wooden embellishments

Lazertran
www.lazertran.com
transfer decal paper

L'il Davis Designs
www.lildavisdesigns.com
chipboard products, foam stamps, embellishments

Magic Scraps
Advantus Corp.
www.magicscraps.com
paper, embellishments, adhesives

Magistical Memories
www.magisticalmemories.com
chipboard alphabets

Making Memories
www.makingmemories.com
paper, foam stamps, paint, embellishments

Maude & Millie
www.maudeandmillie.com
embellishments

Melissa Frances
www.melissafrances.com
paper, embellishments and home décor

Mystic Press
www.mysticpress.com
embellishments

Prima Marketing, Inc.
www.mulberrypaperflowers.com
paper flowers

Provo Craft
www.provocraft.com
embellishments

Quickutz
www.quickutz.com
die-cutting tools and die cuts

Scenic Route
Paper Company
www.scenicroutepaper.com
paper and embellishments

Scrapworks
www.scrapworks.com
paper, embellishments

SEI
www.shopsei.com
scrapbook paper, embellishments

Strathmore
www.mohawkpaper.com
paper products

Wild Asparagus
www.mymindseyeinc.com
scrapbook paper

Yasutomo
www.yasutomo.com
art supplies, paper, embellishments

Stamps and Inks

A Stamp in the Hand
www.astampinthehand.com
rubber stamps

Clearsnap, Inc.
www.clearsnap.com
inks

Fontwerks
www.fontwerks.com
rubber stamps, paper

Hampton Art Stamps
www.hamptonart.com
rubber stamps

Hero Arts
www.heroarts.com
rubber stamps

Inkadinkado
www.inkadinkado.com
rubber stamps

Judi-Kins
www.judikins.com
Diamond Glaze, rubber stamps

Ma Vinci's Reliquary
www.crafts.dm.net/mall/
reliquary
rubber stamps

The Missing Link Stamp Co.
www.missinglinkstamp.com
rubber stamps

Paper Bag Studios
www.paperbagstudios.com
rubber stamps

Ranger Industries
www.rangerink.com
inks

Postmodern Design
Rubber Stamps
(405) 321-3176
rubber stamps

River City Rubber Works
www.rivercityrubberworks.com
*rubber stamps, templates,
embellishments, kits*

Savvy Stamps
www.savvystamps.com
rubber stamps, embellishments

Stampers Anonymous
www.stampersanonymous.com
rubber stamps

Stampington & Co.
www.stampington.com
rubber stamps

Stampotique Originals, Inc.
www.stampotique.com
rubber stamps

Tsukineko Co., Ltd.
www.tsukineko.com
ink

Turtle Press
www.turtlearts.com
rubber stamps

Wendi Speciale Designs
www.wendispeciale.com
rubber stamps

Fabric Supplies

Beacon Chemical Co.
www.beaconcreates.com
fabric stiffening spray

Cranston
www.cranstonvillage.com
fabric

DMC
www.dmc-usa.com
embroidery floss

Jacquard Products
www.jacquardproducts.com
printable fabric

May Arts
www.mayarts.com
ribbon

Maya Road
www.mayaroad.com
ribbon

Michael Miller Memories
www.michaelmillermemories.com
fabric paper, fabric

Midori, Inc.
www.midoriribbon.com
ribbon, paper

Moda Fabrics
www.modafabrics.com
fabrics

Offray
www.offray.com
ribbon

Painting Supplies

Delta Technical Coatings, Inc.
www.deltacrafts.com
craft paint

Fredrix
www.fredrixartistcanvas.com
artist canvas

Golden Artist Colors, Inc.
www.goldenpaints.com
gel mediums, gesso, tar gel

Krylon
www.krylon.com
paint, glazes, finishes

Liquitex
www.liquitex.com
paint products, artist mediums

Nicholson's
Peerless Watercolors
www.peerlesscolor.com
watercolors

Additional Supplies

Amaco
www.amaco.com
paint, finishes, clay and tools

Avery Office Products
www.avery.com
*office supplies, adhesives,
school supplies, ink*

Club Scrap
www.clubscrap.com
paper cording techniques

Creative Paperclay Company
www.paperclay.com
paper clay

Daylab
www.daylab.com
*Daylab equipment
and accessories*

Duncan Enterprises
www.duncancrafts.com
tacky glue

Eclectic Products, Inc.
www.eclecticproducts.com
E6000 glue

Grafix
www.grafixarts.com
self-adhesive transparencies

Lineco/Books By Hand
www.lineco.com
PVA glue, book board

My Fonts
www.myfonts.com
fonts

Plaid Enterprises, Inc
www.plaidonline.com
craft paint, Mod Podge

Prym-Dritz
www.dritz.com
grommets (large)

Sakura
www.gellyroll.com
pens and art mediums

Saunders
www.saunders-usa.com
UHU glue stick

Silver Crow Creations
www.silvercrowcreations.com
gifts, stamps, art supplies

Tandy Leather Factory
www.tandyleather.com
*leather, tools,
metal embellishments*

Technique Tuesdays
www.techniquetuesdays.com
*clear stamps, ink pads,
acrylic blocks, accessories*

Timeless Touches
Dove Valley Productions
www.timelesstouches.net
fibers, templates, tools

Tombow Adhesive
www.tombowusa.com
adhesive products

USArtQuest, Inc.
www.usartquest.com
*metal embellishments,
Perfect Paper Adhesive*

Walnut Hollow
www.walnuthollow.com
wood products

Westrim Crafts
www.westrimcrafts.com
board books, embellishments

Index

A

Accordion books, 62, 74, 79
Adhesives, 10
Alphabet fabric, 55
Alphabet letters, 102
Alphadotz, 109
Antiquing polish, 19
The Arboretum, 104
Art File, 96
Artists, 121
Ashley Then and Now, 119
Awl, 10, 28, 117

B

Binder's board, 10
Blanket stitch, 89, 123
Bloom and Grow, 39
Bone folder, 10
Book Arts, 60
    Entrances, 90
    Family Deck, 68
    Gallery, 94
    Imagine, 86
    Japanese stab binding books, 90
    The Love of Color, 82
    metal books, 87
    Oh, Bandana!, 78
    100% You, 62
    Organized Chaos, 64—67
    She's Got Hatitude!, 74
    This and That, 70
Book board, 10
Book cloth, 10
Bookmaking Techniques, 122
    blanket stitch, 89, 123
    covering book board, 122
    pamphlet stitch, 80, 123
    supplies, 10
Brayer, 10, 116
Bristle brush, 8, 15
Buttons, 26

C

Cabinet doors, 104
Cardboard, 14, 73
Cardstock, 8, 77
Ceramics, 110
Childhood Food Traditions, 94
Chipboard, 8, 37
Clipboard book, 64
Cording, 20, 21
Cousins, 110
Cover board, 10
Covering book board, 122

D

Daylab, 114
Diamond Glaze, 10, 20
Die cuts, 46

E

E6000 adhesive, 10
Tote bag, 63
Transparent art, 85
Emotions in artwork, 7
Enjoying Life, 58
Entrances, 90

F

Fabric arts, 44
    Family, 46
    Gallery, 58
    I Love..., 48
    My Ancestry: the Children, 54
    Summer Memories, 50
    Yes, You Are a Princess, 52
Fabric
    alphabet, 55
    fabric paper, 59
    fabric stiffening spray, 10, 46—47
    printable, 10
    resources, 125
    supplies, 10
Family, 46

G

Family 4 Each Other, 34
Family Deck, 68
Family Photo Boxes, 41
Flip-Flop Girls, 14
Foam core, 17
Forever Friends, 16

G

Gaffer's tape, 10
Gel medium, 8, 55, 56, 106
Generations, 30
Gesso, 8, 36
Gluing on, 56

H

Handwriting, 32—33

I

I Love..., 48
Ilse and the Lion Cub, 100
Imagine, 86
Imperial Beach, 24
Inks, 33, 84, 124
Iron on, 49
It's a Girl Thing, 95

J

Just Friends Having Fun, 58

L

Lazertran transfer paper, 8, 40, 108, 112
Life, 102
Little Things, 32
Love of Color, The, 82
Love...by Example, 22

M

Memories of Rome, 43
Memory artist, 7

Mini books, 37, 52
Mod Podge, 10, 31
Mother and Daughter Bridesmaids, 42
Multimedia, 108
My Ancestry: the Children, 54
My Girl for All Seasons, 118
My Sister, My Friend, 38
My Tribute to Grandpop, 26

N
No Day Like Today, 120

O
Office space, 66
Oh, Bandana!, 78
100% You, 62
Organized Chaos, 64

P
Painting supplies, 8, 125
Pamphlet stitch, 80, 123
Paper Arts, 12
    Family 4 Each Other, 34
    Flip-Flop Girls, 14
    Forever Friends, 16
    Gallery, 38
    Generations, 30
    Imperial Beach, 24
    Little Things, 32
    Love...by Example, 22
    My Tribute to Grandpop, 26
    Steven and Mr. Gecko, 20
Papers
    fabric paper, 59
    Lazertran transfer paper, 8, 40, 108, 112
    paper clay, 28
    papier mâché, 30, 34, 101
    resources, 124
    tissue paper, 31
    watercolor, 24–25

Parisian Reflections, 40
Perfect Paper Adhesive (PPA), 10
Photo cropping, 15, 105
Plastic slide holder page, 73
Polaroid image transfer, 114–117
Postcards, 50
Pure, 38
PVA adhesive, 10

R
Regular gel medium, 8, 55
Remembering to Laugh, 42
Resources, 124
Road Trip of a Lifetime, The, 43

S
Samantha, 106
Scratch art, 96
She's All Girl, 108
She's Got Hattitude!, 74
Shy Beauty, 114
Simply You, 40
Smile Like You Mean It, 59
Soft gel medium, 8, 56
Stamps, 18, 37, 77, 105, 124
Steven and Mr. Gecko, 20
Summer Memories, 50
Supplies, 8, 124

T
Tacky glue, 10
Tassels, paper, 29
Thickness of pages, 72
This and That, 70
Tied, 59
Tissue paper, 31
Tools for cutting, poking, and smoothing, 10
Tote bag, 62
Transfer mediums, 8, 54–57, 112
Transparency pages, 33
Transparent art, 82, 106

U
UHU glue stick, 10

W
Wall Arts, 98
    Arboretum, The, 104
    Cousins, 110
    Gallery, 118
    Ilse and the Lion Cub, 100
    Life, 102
    Samantha, 106
    She's All Girl, 108
    Shy Beauty, 114
Watercolor paints and paper, 24
Weaving, paper, 22

Y
Yes, You Are a Princess, 52
Your Future, 39

Find artful inspiration in these other North Light titles!

Collage Discovery Workshop: Beyond the Unexpected
by Claudine Hellmuth

ISBN-10: 1-58180-678-7, ISBN-13: 978-1-58180-678-6,
paperback, 128 pages, #33267

In a follow-up to her first workshop book, Claudine Hellmuth taps into a whole new level of creativity in *Beyond the Unexpected*. Inside you'll find original artwork and inventive ideas that show you how to personalize your own collage pieces using new techniques and interesting surfaces. In addition, the extensive gallery compiled by Claudine and other top collage artists will spark your imagination. Whether you're a beginner or a collage veteran, you'll enjoy this lovely book both as inspiration and as a practical guide.

The Artful Card
by Alison Eads

ISBN-10: 1-58180-680-9, ISBN-13: 978-1-58180-680-9,
paperback, 128 pages, #33269

The Artful Card showcases over 25 gorgeous cards and keepsakes made with collage techniques using printed papers, embellishments and found objects. With her unique, romantic style and simple yet clever techniques, Alison Eads brings the hottest trends in scrapbooking to the cardmaking world. Whether you're making a romantic card for your someone special, or you just want to send a friend or family member a handmade message to show you care, you're sure to find just the right thing inside *The Artful Card*.

Sew Easy Papercrafting
by Rebekah Meier

ISBN-10: 1-58180-772-4, ISBN-13: 978-1-58180-772-1,
paperback, 128 pages, #33444

In *Sew Easy Papercrafting*, author Rebekah Meier takes you beyond the scrapbook page and shows you how to use fabric, sewing and sewing notions to create 20 beautiful, vintage-style papercrafting projects. Inside, you'll learn step by step how to create fabulous paper-based projects, from fabric-embellished greeting cards and felt- and lace-covered journals, to paper "crazy quilt" file folders and fabric tag books. With their embellishments of ribbon, bows, buttons and scrapbook charms, each of the projects has a warm, vintage look you'll love.

Fresh Ideas in Découpage
by Colette George

ISBN-10: 1-58180-655-8, ISBN-13: 978-1-58180-655-7,
paperback, 128 pages, #33242

Fresh Ideas in Découpage shows you how to create handmade decorative accessories infused with your personal style. Each project teaches you techniques for creating pieces with the layered and textured detail found in your favorite home décor shop but with tips and hints for making the piece your own. Inside *Fresh Ideas in Découpage*, you'll find over 25 step-by-step and variation projects that will help you turn your home into a show room. Each project will teach you simple yet sophisticated techniques, such as how to layer paint, wax, plaster, stain and even ink to create elegant finished pieces.

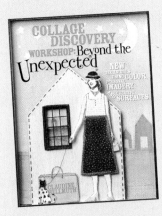

These and other fine North Light titles are available from your local art and craft retailer, bookstore or online supplier.